U-BOAT HUNTERS
Cornwall's Air War
1916 -1919

PETER LONDON

DYLLANSOW TRURAN

Other titles by Peter London

Saunders and Saro Aircraft since 1917 (Putnam 1988)
Aviation in Cornwall (Air-Britain 1997)
RNAS Culdrose (Alan Sutton 1999)

First Published by Dyllansow Truran
Croft Prince, Mount Hawke, Truro TR4 8EE

ISBN   1 85022 135 9

Printed and bound in Cornwall by R Booth (Bookbinder) Ltd & Troutbeck Press
Antron Hill, Mabe, Penryn TR10 9HH

Main text set in Novarese

Acknowledgements
I would like to acknowledge with gratitude the kind help, generosity and practical support I have received from the following people and institutions during the production of this history:

Bob Andrew, Chris Ashworth, Paddy Bradley, Jack Bruce, Bude Museum, Brian Butcher, Cornish Studies Library, Redruth (Terry Knight and Kim Cooper), Robert A Dorrien-Smith, *Falmouth Packet*, Fleet Air Arm Museum (Dave Richards), Frank Gibson, Lt Malcolm Goram, Helston Folk Museum (Martin Matthews and Janet Spargo), Stuart Leslie, Tony Maasz, Malcolm McCarthy, Ces Mowthorpe, the staff of the Penzance Subscription Library, the staff of the Public Libraries at Bodmin, Penzance,
Falmouth and Truro, the staff of the Public Records Office, Thornley Renfree, Royal Institution of Cornwall (Roger Penhallurick), Royal Cornwall Polytechnic Society Research Project (Peter Gilson), Royal Naval Air Station Culdrose, Hugh Sheridan, Ian Stratfield, Ray Sturtivant, Dennis Teague, Stanley Tonkin, *West Briton*, *Western Morning News*, Reg Watkiss, Peter Wearne, Bruce Wood, Bill Young.

The cramped car of Royal Naval Air Service Coastal Airship C.9, in flight, summer 1916. Her pilot, Flight Lieutenant J G Struthers, is in the foreground wearing flying helmet and goggles. To his right, a Lewis machine-gun mounting and a large camera are positioned. Behind him, the radio operator has donned his headset while in the aft position is a third crew member. C.9 was based at Royal Naval Air Station Mullion from June 1916 until October 1918. (Ian Stratford collection).

FRONT COVER:
Sopwith 1½ Strutter two-seat fighter N5624 at Royal Naval Air Station Mullion, situated on the western side of Cornwall's Lizard peninsula. The pilot and observer are both aboard. The ground crew makes ready to start the engine and release the wheel chocks, while a Flight Lieutenant with arms folded stands by the fuselage of the machine. Behind the Sopwith is a windbreak used to screen the larger of Mullion's airship sheds, its structure covered with corrugated cladding. This photograph was taken during the fleeting visit of N5624 to Mullion in April 1917. (J M Bruce/G S Leslie collection).

This book is dedicated to my dear old Dad, AG.

Peter London has written on aviation for fifteen years. He is a regular contributor to the aviation press and is author of three previous books on the subject. He has researched aviation in Cornwall for ten years and is a member of the Cornish Aviation Society. He is married to Joanne and works in the defence industry.

Contents

Introduction   1
    1   The Campaign - Background
    2   The Airship Genre

Part One - Cornwall's Airships
    1   Beginnings   7
    2   The Coastals   11
    3   Expansion   15
    4   Action   21
    5   The SSZ Class   34
    6   Mullion's Own Airship   40

Part Two - The Aircraft Deterrent
    1   Mullion, and New Stations   47
    2   Operations and Accidents   60

Part Three - Aftermath
    1   The War Ends   73
    2   Remains   75

Appendices
Appendix 1:   RNAS/RAF airfield and airship station command structure
          in Cornwall and the Isles of Scilly, to 1919   79
Appendix 2:   Locations of airfields, airship stations and aircraft storage depots
          in Cornwall and the Isles of Scilly, 1916 - 19   80
Appendix 3:   Summary of aircraft Flights and Squadrons operating from
          Cornwall and the Isles of Scilly, 1917 - 19   85
Appendix 4:   Individual aircraft known to have operated from
          Cornwall and the Isles of Scilly, 1917 - 19   86
Appendix 5:   Individual airships operating from RNAS Mullion, 1916 - 1919   87
Appendix 6:   RNAS Tresco - sorties by individual aircraft   88
Appendix 7:   Areas patrolled by RNAS aircraft and airships operating from
          Cornwall and the Isles of Scilly   89
Appendix 8:   RNAS rank structure and Royal Flying Corps equivalents   90
Appendix 9:   Specifications of airship types operating from Cornwall, 1916 - 19   91
Appendix 10:   Specifications of aircraft types operating from Cornwall and the Isles of
          Scilly, 1916 - 19   92

INTRODUCTION

I THE CAMPAIGN - BACKGROUND

Prior to 1916, the people of Cornwall saw little flying activity. During the early part of the century the county was among the most remote areas of Britain, and far from the centres where the development and growth of aviation were taking place. The first aeroplane to make a visit to Cornwall had arrived at Penzance during July 1910, a flimsy Farman biplane which carried out exhibition flights from a field just east of the town, piloted by one of Britain's leading pioneer aviators of the day, Claude Grahame-White. April 1912 witnessed a call by the Frenchman Henri Salmet, flying a Bleriot monoplane, while Briton Gustav Hamel visited briefly during September 1913, also bringing a Bleriot - the first person to fly to the Land's End. In April 1914 Henri Salmet returned, using a Bleriot capable of conversion from wheeled to float undercarriage and in June of that year Lord John Carbery travelled to Redruth on his Morane Type G two-seat monoplane for an exhibition. These early flights were incredibly popular, of course, and were attended by thousands of Cornish men and women, but the outbreak of the First World War in August 1914 put a prompt end to civilian flying.

However, the strategic position of the county at the conjunction of the Atlantic Ocean and the English Channel saw to it that during the War, the aeronautical isolation previously experienced by Cornwall came to an end. As 1914 drew towards a close it became clear that despite all hopes, hostilities would not be over by Christmas. The more industrialised of the combatant nations accelerated the process of exploiting the technology of the day, in ever more complex and innovative attempts to attain the advantage over the enemy.

One of the most formidable of the weapons deployed by either side during the First World War was the *Unterseeboot*, or U-boat submarine used by the Imperial German Navy. As the war continued, these craft were developed and their building programmes were greatly increased. They were given unlimited licence to maraud the sea lanes upon which rested the continued ability of Britain to fight. In turn, rural Cornwall quickly became host to the airships and later, aeroplanes of the Royal Naval Air Service (RNAS), which were sent to help counter the U-boat menace in the Channel and the Western Approaches.

This is the story of the aerial campaign fought from Cornwall's shores, the men who flew and supported the RNAS aircraft and airships based there, and their actions which contributed towards turning the tide in the relentless struggle against Germany's submarines.

2 THE AIRSHIP GENRE

The airship has its ancestry in the balloon and dates back to the 1890s, when the fundamental technical steps came together of modifying the classical 'onion' shape of the balloon's gas-bag (or envelope) into a more streamlined profile with a distinct fore-and-aft, while attaching an efficient, lightweight engine driving a propeller, and providing steering equipment generally in the form of aft-mounted rudders and elevators. These developments allowed the new type of craft to overcome the severe operational strictures of the balloon, which if not tethered is entirely at the mercy of wind speed and direction. The first successful airship was designed and built by the Brazilian pioneer Alberto Santos Dumont, and first flew during 1898; in September 1905, Ernest T Willows flew the first such practical British craft. Airship development continued apace

during the Edwardian period, notably in Germany under Count Von Zeppelin, but also in France and to a lesser extent Britain.

Three distinct forms of airships evolved, though all varieties employed hydrogen as the lifting agent, for helium, though it held the considerable advantage of being an inert gas, was very rare and expensive at that time. The Royal Naval Air Service relied mostly upon non-rigid airships, which

Left. Coastal Star Class airship C*6 reveals her underside and beamy trilobe envelope over RNAS Mullion. She wears national markings on her flight control surfaces. The ground crew has split into two groups to catch the guy ropes released from the airship, and thereby assist the craft to land. In the background is visible Mullion's circular practice bombing area, cut into the scrub on the south-western side of the station. This photograph was taken during the autumn of 1918. (Tony Maasz)

Below. SSZ Class airship from Mullion seen from the eastern end of Boscawen Street, Truro, during the summer or autumn of 1918. (Royal Institution of Cornwall)

were the simplest and smallest of the airship types. In this class, the gas envelope was of treated fabric, its shape maintained not by any form of internal structure, but by keeping the hydrogen within at a somewhat greater pressure than the surrounding air. This differential was achieved by installing large bags or ballonets inside the envelope, containing air which was forced in or released as needed, in order to maintain the required pressure within the hydrogen-filled majority of the envelope as the airship rose or descended. The pressure was also regulated by automatic valves in the envelope, which allowed hydrogen to escape should it rise above the desired amount.

The pressure of the hydrogen within the envelope naturally rose relative to the surrounding air as the airship ascended. If this situation was allowed to continue unabated, the valves would blow at the point where the envelope's internal pressure was at the prescribed limit, and hydrogen would be lost. Depending on the amount of hydrogen released in this way, the result when descending would be a degree of deflation and a loss of shape of the envelope, which in turn would result in impaired or loss of control of the airship.

In practice therefore, in order to retain a constant amount of hydrogen within the envelope, as the airship rose, the air in the ballonets was released until they were completely deflated; at that point the airship was said to be at its 'pressure height', where any further ascent would mean loss of hydrogen through the valves. If necessary greater altitude could be made, but only if hydrogen were released. The ballonet air valves were designed to blow off at a slightly lower pressure than the hydrogen valves. The refilling of the ballonets when the airship was descending was carried out by means of special air blowers or by air scoops situated in the slipstream of its engine propellers. Usually two or more ballonets were employed, in order to enable the trim of the vessel to be controlled to some extent.

Of the other classes of airship, the rigid was the largest variety, and relied on a light metal framework containing multiple gas-bags, while a third class was a technical compromise between the rigid and the non-rigid types, employing ballonets but also a keel along the bottom of the envelope to provide enhanced rigidity and weight distribution. Airship gondolas were swiftly developed, replacing the basket of the balloon and suspended by rigging below the envelope, often of a size to allow several persons to fly and, as military applications developed, carriage of weaponry - compared with the aircraft of the day, airships were formidable load-carriers.

Handling the airship on the ground presented a number of particular difficulties. Because they were huge and comparatively light, airships could be severely affected by even gentle winds, and great care had to be taken to ensure they were not accidentally blown across their stations and damaged. To accommodate them, vast sheds were built, adjacent to areas of flat land which did not need to provide any form of runway in the conventional sense, but were nonetheless essential for the necessary manoeuvring of the vessels. Into and out of the sheds, the airships were gingerly walked by large teams of ground crew, sometimes up to a hundred men, using handling guy-ropes. To effect a take-off the airship was taken a safe distance from its shed across the open area by the handling crew, then swung into wind with engines running, and the guys released on command. When landing, the airship would manoeuvre very slowly upwind at a low altitude, while trailing the handling guys, or in poor conditions a heavy trail rope, ready for the handling party to catch, whereupon the vessel would be walked carefully back to its shed.

The sheds also provided the shelter in which maintenance could be carried out. The airships' envelopes were periodically deflated and carefully inspected for damage and leaks. They were then repaired, or sometimes replaced entirely. Their engines, used in missions sometimes in excess of twenty hours' duration, had frequently to be overhauled, while the rigging too, was routinely subjected to close scrutiny.

An alternative to the shed, which was occasionally adopted, was the airship mooring mast. While it provided no covered accommodation for the airship, the mast, to which the vessel was attached by the nose of its envelope, allowed it to swing with changes of wind direction, which in turn served to protect it from the possible damage such winds might cause were it simply to be moored to the ground facing in a fixed direction. In addition to its considerable economy compared with the provision of a shed, the mast had the advantage that only a small ground crew was needed to operate it, there being no necessity for the airship to be manoeuvred by a large handling party. Even in reasonably high winds it was comparatively straightforward for the airship to be launched from a mast by simply slipping its moorings.

As for the crews who flew the airships, they were volunteers to a man, often recruited from the Royal Naval Volunteer Reserve (RNVR) as well as from the RNAS. Their training in the art of airship flight was very brief and consisted of a handful of balloon ascents, a few hours on small training airships, followed by a posting to a war station where they picked up the real techniques of flying operationally. They were obliged to adapt very quickly to a brand new form of warfare requiring many special skills, and they were not found wanting.

Coastal Airship C.2 being walked into Mullion's larger shed following a patrol. Evidently no sightings had been made of submarines, for the bombload is intact. A Lewis gun can be seen mounted on the aft landing skid, while a large camera is mounted on the starboard side of the car. An engineer stands on the external footrail in order to tend to the aft engine. (Kind permission RNAS Culdrose)

Above. Sea Scout Zero Class Airship SSZ.40 at Mullion, with attendant ground crew. The craft is under power and is positioned at the northern end of the station. (J M Bruce/G S Leslie collection)

Below. Coastal C2 is manoeuvred across the open ground at Mullion by a considerable handling party. The groups either side of the craft give the appearance of pulling against each other, but may be in the process of turning the airship. (Helston Folk Museum)

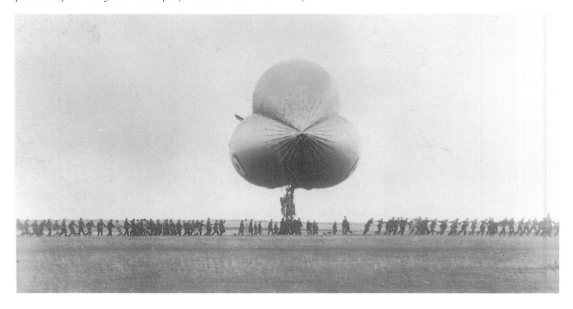

PART ONE
CORNWALL'S AIRSHIPS

1 BEGINNINGS

The summer of 1914 was marked by sharply increasing international tension and anxiety as the peoples of Europe waited, vainly, for a halt in the slide toward war. In Britain, civilian aviation, which had bloomed over the previous few years, came to a swift end as aircraft and resources were hastily gathered together during August at the onset of hostilities, to support the military expedition to France. As the campaign continued into the autumn, the Belgian Channel ports Ostende and Zeebrugge fell to enemy forces and their maritime facilities were occupied by the Imperial German Navy.

The acquisition of these ports allowed the Germans the opportunity to increase the use of their *Unterseebooten*, or U-boats. At that time, Britain was dependent on the import of huge quantities of food and raw materials in order to live, let alone wage war, and all such supplies naturally came by sea, so the potential of the U-boat to influence the progress of the war was profound. Initially the Germans deployed their submarines only against warships but soon merchant and passenger craft became targets in addition to Royal Navy vessels. As early as 2 September 1914, the small but

Spring 1917 at RNAS Mullion; the building work has scarred the landscape. The main airship shed is complete except for the observation tower that was later placed above its main doors, and the wind-breaks have been erected. The mouth of the shed faces the prevailing south-west wind. To the right, preparations are in hand to erect a smaller second shed, and workmen can be seen. A tiny railway line serves the construction work on the second site. A single Sopwith 1½ Strutter biplane is visible to the lower left, and a party of men to the lower right. (Author's collection)

deadly U-21 commanded by *Kapitänleutnant* Hersing crept up the Firth of Forth before being detected near the Forth Bridge, and safely withdrew before torpedoing HMS *Pathfinder* the following day, which sank in four minutes; 259 of her crew were lost.

In the early hours of New Year's Day 1915 the battleship HMS *Formidable* was torpedoed off Lyme Regis by the U-24, and 547 died. British newspapers were obliged by the Government to resist reporting the location of the sinking because it had taken place very much in home waters and underlined the effectiveness and intrusive capability of the enemy's weapon. Early that year too, the U-boats commenced operations in the western Channel and in the Irish Sea; at the end of January, the U-21 surfaced off Barrow-in-Furness and shelled the airship shed there, the first appearance of a U-boat off the west coast of Britain. On 4 February Germany announced a policy of indiscriminate submarine warfare in all waters around the British Isles, including the Channel, under which all enemy shipping encountered would be attacked, while it was also made clear that neutral vessels entered those waters at their peril. This policy came into force on 18 February. During the course of just one day, 12 March, the U-29 sank four vessels off the Isles of Scilly. Later, on 7 May, the Cunard liner *Lusitania* was torpedoed and sank with the loss of some 1,200 lives, of which 124 were American citizens. The unrestricted submarine campaign was to continue until April 1916 when neutral America presented an ultimatum to Germany, threatening to end diplomatic relations following the sinking of the Channel packet *Sussex*, again with a number of Americans aboard.

Coastal Class airship C.9, its engines stopped and with a large ground-handling crew in attendance, returns to its shed at Mullion during the summer of 1916. Its ballonet air scoop is located in the forward position. In the distance is a second Coastal. Visible too is a shed windbreak in the course of construction. (J M Bruce/G S Leslie collection)

The grave situation caused the British Admiralty to conduct an understandably urgent examination into possible counters to the U-boat. It was concluded that anti-U-boat patrols would best be carried out using not only surface vessels but also a network of airships based at strategic points around the British Isles and operated by the Royal Naval Air Service (RNAS). Following the recommendations of the Air Committee, a body appointed during 1912 by the Committee of Imperial Defence, from 1 January 1914 control of all British airships used for military purposes had passed to the Admiralty's Naval Wing of the Royal Flying Corps, as the RNAS had then been officially known, and so by the time the Admiralty conducted its deliberations, the attributes of the *genre* were well appreciated by those charged with providing an answer to the U-boat menace.

The Admiralty's decision to proceed with the design and construction of airships with which to help oppose the German submarines was formally agreed on 28 February 1915. It was considered the U-boats would be somewhat easier to spot from the air than from sea level, while even early airships were capable of great endurance and range, and could be easily adapted to carry bombs. Installation of wireless equipment would allow co-operation with the ships of the Royal Navy so as to be able to harmonise attacks on sighted submarines. Following the Admiralty's conclusions, a number of sites were identified at which to commence the building of airship stations around the British coastline. The new stations came under the command of the RNAS, and the initial phase of the building process continued through 1915 and well into 1916. This development led to the arrival of the service in Cornwall, and marked the onset of an aerial presence there which remained until after the Armistice.

The slow speed and poor manoeuvrability of the airship compared with the aircraft of the day of course made it potentially very vulnerable to attack from that quarter. It was recognised that the offensive capability of the aeroplane, almost non-existent at the time of the Admiralty's deliberations, would increase rapidly as war accelerated the progress of destructive technology. Indeed, both sides had already experimented with aerial handguns and rifles; much more importantly, the Germans were well on the way to fielding the machine-gun interrupter gear in their Fokker E.1 monoplane scout, while the Royal Flying Corps was busily adopting a series of FE pusher biplanes, also armed with machine-guns. The Admiralty acknowledged that, in the longer-term, as such developments continued, the deployment of airships would have to be confined strictly to areas where German aviators were not present.

However, for operations distanced from any opposing aerial activity the airship was quite suitable, and given the modest ranges of contemporary aeroplanes there were clearly huge areas around the British Isles where such a weapon could be safely brought to bear. The principles of airship design and construction were well advanced, and work quickly began on new types with which to populate the emerging stations. Flying and maintenance training was instated in the new craft, while the development continued of radio direction finding equipment. The chain of RNAS bases envisaged by the Admiralty eventually stretched from the west coast of Scotland, around the Irish Sea and the English Channel, along the North Sea coastline and north to the Orkney Islands.

*

The Cornish village of Mullion is situated on the south-western side of the Lizard peninsula, which itself forms the most southerly part of Britain. Like much of Cornwall the area is isolated, of great natural beauty and subject to sudden and dramatic changes in weather. Mullion nestles on a shoreline which has witnessed the passing Spanish Armada, and Napoleon's navies; its position near the western entry to the English Channel is strategically critical.

During mid 1916, the waters off Cornwall's coastline became host to a bitter battle which was prosecuted without quarter until the war's end, as airship and U-boat began a struggle to press home their very different advantages. The Lizard, protruding deeply into the Channel, was clearly a very attractive location for an airship site from which to provide aerial cover over the surrounding seas, at least in terms of physical location, although the land there is very exposed and from time to time is afflicted by fierce winds and rain. Notwithstanding the capricious climate, however, Royal Naval Air Station Mullion (initially known as Lizard Airship Station) was formally commissioned during June 1916. The new base consisted of 320 acres of flat land belonging to the Bonython estate off the Cross Lanes to Newton road, immediately east of and abutting the Bonython Plantations, adjacent to the small village of Cury and north-east of Mullion itself. Its simple postal address was 'Mullion RN Airship Station, Cury Cross Lanes, South Cornwall'.

Building work at Mullion had commenced during March 1916. The construction programme was marked at its onset by local irritation resulting from the arrival of the numerous RNAS lorries employed to deliver equipment and materials to the site. Heavy and slow, the noisy lorries disturbed the nearby livestock and damaged the roads in the area, many of which were little more than tracks and quite unsuitable for such vehicles. Relations with the civilian populace became further strained when one of the lorries was in collision with a pedestrian (though it was later suggested the pedestrian had been 'in drink'), while another clattered into and broke down a fence at the perimeter of a small-holding, providing several pigs with a temporary taste of freedom. In addition to these incidents, a serious accident took place on site during March; engineer's labourer William Carter was inclining a heavy wooden frame when it fell and killed him.

Workers living nearby were hired for much of the site clearance work and for the erection of the less complex buildings, particularly the wooden accommodation huts. The labour requisitions necessary to facilitate this caused friction with the surrounding landowners, who felt the comparatively few men remaining in the area would be much better employed in agricultural jobs - many had of course departed for the services. During mid-May indeed, in a fit of radical thinking the Truro Urban War Service Committee meeting held at the Town Hall contemplated the use of women on the land, in order to help solve the problem of the lack of men available for agricultural work, and the food shortage it was felt might result thereby. This was one of many such meetings held in Cornwall (and elsewhere) and considerable concern was expressed over the ever-dwindling male labour supply. Little could the objectors know that the Mullion station had a most important life ahead, becoming the centre of airship operations in Cornwall and indeed the south-west during the First World War, and growing to be one of the busiest bases in the nation-wide RNAS network.

Mullion's airship shed was built by A & J Main Ltd of Glasgow and when completed was a vast 358 ft in length, with a clear span of 110 ft and a clear height of 75 ft. Local contracts were let for the manoeuvring of some of the materials on site, including the components of the huge steel frames necessary for the shed, and this was usually carried out by teams of horses. Once the frames were assembled, they were positioned using two 10-ton travelling cranes, and the resulting structure clad with corrugated metal sheeting. On the combing of the shed roof line was mounted an observation tower, while the hydrogen supply pipeline for the airships was routed through the concrete flooring. The design featured huge sliding doors at both ends, which were so heavy they were often opened and closed by tractors rather than by teams of men. The shed was built facing into the prevailing south-westerly wind in order to ensure the launching of its charges was as straightforward as possible, and was comfortably able to accommodate two of the Coastal Class airships intended for service from the station. Though Mullion was commissioned during June 1916, the building work carried on well into the following year.

Screening protection for the entrances of the shed was provided in the form of towering windbreaks mounted on concrete blocks and supported by heavy bracing structures, designed to mask the airships from unwanted winds during the manoeuvres involved in moving them in and out. A Silicol hydrogen-producing plant and gasometer, a secure area for the high-pressure gas bottles, electricity generator, engine shop, wireless cabin and meteorological hut were swiftly built. The wireless cabin employed a Marconi $^1/_2$ kw transmitter powered by a $2^3/_4$ hp Douglas engine. The Silicol plant was later replaced by a more up-to-date water/steam/iron gas plant.

While billets for the majority of officers were prepared in the surrounding villages and hamlets, accommodation for the ratings at Mullion was built on the station itself, in the form of wooden huts, and a canteen was quickly erected, the domestic buildings being situated at the northern end of the site. A YMCA hut also appeared there, funded by the donation of £150 from the Helston and District Allies' Relief Fund Committee and erected by Mr Bennett of Bodmin under a contract let in mid-May.

Despite the enormous and clearly visible airship shed erected over the early summer, the arrival of its huge occupants, the accompanying building work and all the associated disruption running counter to the previous rural tranquillity of the Lizard, the Cornish press had virtually nothing to say regarding the establishment of Mullion. All newspapers were obliged to act in accordance with the strict censorship orders of the day prescribed by the ubiquitous intrusion of DORA, the Defence of the Realm Act, which had been promulgated at the onset of war. This lack of publicity was of course completely unable to mask activities from the curious eyes of nearby residents, and vivid rumours abounded as to the types of activity allegedly carried out by the station. Clandestine night-time missions into the enemy territory beyond the Channel were envisaged (by the locals), though in some quarters the view was expressed that the arriving RNAS personnel had been given a soft option compared with the experiences of those fighting in France. However, the courage and determination of the Mullion airship men was repeatedly demonstrated and the surrounding civilians, never susceptible to sudden change, grew to respect and admire what they learned of their new neighbours' work.

During late August 1916 an opportunity arose for locals and new arrivals to get to know each other when the station contributed personnel to the local annual concert in aid of the Lizard Lifeboat Fund, and a number of RNAS men took part in singing, playing the pianoforte and conjuring tricks. Foremost among the entertainers were Chief Petty Officer Oakes the comedian (an unusual combination?) and Air Mechanic Longden, who performed on the piano. This concert was followed at the end of October by a similar event at the Godolphin Hall in Helston under Lieutenant-Commander Blair, in aid of the Trafalgar Day Fund for Orphans of Seamen and Marines, which was well attended and a great success. Such events continued throughout the RNAS residence on the Lizard and eventually a full station band was formed at Mullion. Its personnel were frequently excused the more mundane duties associated with service life and so the band rapidly attracted a considerable membership. Mullion's musicians received much praise from those who attended the various village fêtes and functions at which the band performed.

2 THE COASTALS

The first airship posted to RNAS Mullion was one of the new Coastal Class, numbered C.8, which began its journey to Cornwall from Kingsnorth, a base controlled by the RNAS near Hoo on the River Medway, during May of 1916, even before the first phase of the building work at the new station had been finished. Unfortunately though, C.8 never arrived in the Duchy, crashing in the sea off Start

Its engines stopped, C.9 is manhandled across Mullion's scrub by its ground crew. This job was made particularly difficult in windy conditions, which unfortunately are experienced frequently on The Lizard. (RCPS Research Project)

Point, Devon, and being struck off charge on 9 June. Three of those aboard died, including the captain, Flt Lt Dickinson; only the Wireless/Telegraphy (W/T) Operator survived. The reason for the crash of C.8 was never identified, for the lone survivor was unable to explain the cause - possibly whatever took place happened too quickly for him to assimilate. It has been suggested the problem was fuel starvation but this seems unlikely; engine failure in an airship does not mean it must land at once, for such craft can remain aloft for a time through the lift provided by the envelope. In fact the first airship to arrive at Mullion was transported to nearby Helston by railway, using the tortuous branch line opened in 1887 off the main Truro - Penzance route. This was Coastal Class C.9, which first flew from its new base on 18 June and commenced its first operational patrol on 1 July.

The design of the C Class non-rigid airship type was created from the combination of an improvised open car (or gondola) constructed from two Avro aircraft forward fuselages joined back-to-back, mated to a trilobe envelope layout taken from the old *Astra Torres* No 10 airship commissioned in early 1915; indeed the prototype Coastal Class used the actual envelope of No 10. In all, thirty-five examples were built, each at Kingsnorth.

The production C Class employed an envelope of 196 ft in length and a capacity of 170,000 cu ft. It was hydrogen-filled and was made of rubber-proofed fabric doped to increase their weatherproofing and to help effect gas-tightness. The advantage of adopting a trilobe section envelope was that it allowed the car to be slung closer to the envelope than would otherwise have been possible with such a large airship, reducing head resistance and somewhat simplifying the process of maintenance (in terms of access to the envelope) when on the ground. The envelope was kept firm and in shape by means of four ballonets, internal bags into which air was pumped in order to maintain the pressure within the envelope, the bags being fed via an aluminium air scoop situated in the slipstream of the forward propeller. The nose of the envelope was reinforced against the pressure of the wind during forward movement through the use of canes inserted into sleeves, these meeting at an aluminium fabric-covered nose-cap. For steering and stabilising purposes, the vertical fin with the rudder and the horizontal fins with the elevators were set at the aft end of the envelope, while eight main handling guy, plus trail and grappling ropes were provided for manoeuvring the airship on the ground.

The Coastals were powered by two engines, a pusher and a tractor, situated one each end of the car. Usually these were 150 hp water-cooled Sunbeams, though some examples employed a 220 hp Renault in the aft position, while others substituted a 100 hp Berliet in the forward position.

The car of C.9 viewed in Mullion's main airship shed, revealing the locations of its Lewis machine-gun mountings, and bomb mountings. Four bombs are visible. The structure of the car is fabric-covered. In order to move around the car in flight, the crew would step over the side and use the external foot rail which the rating is holding. (RCPS Research Project)

A 1¾ hp ABC motor was also carried, used to power the W/T Operator's generator and in emergency to power an auxiliary blower to feed the ballonets. Two fuel tanks each of 110 gallons were usually mounted next to the engines, but if the Renault engine was used, it was necessary to relocate the aft fuel tank to a position above the engineer's cockpit. The car also contained the engines' compressed air starters and the oil tanks, while the ballast bags were originally designed to carry water, but later modified to contain sand. Tandem landing skids were employed, rather than any conventional form of undercarriage. Usually a complement of five crew was carried, though sometimes six members were preferred. Duties were Pilot, Coxswain, Observer, W/T Operator and Mechanic/ Engineer.

The attachment of the car to the envelope through the use of rigging was very simple and consisted of nine suspension points per side, each branching into bridles; each of these were in turn supported at their termination by further bridles. The final attachment from the bridles to the envelope was by means of *Eta* patches, a system pioneered by the early British airship of that name, consisting of metal D-shaped fittings around which the rigging was spliced and through which a number of webbing bands passed in fan-like shape, being attached in turn to the envelope skinning.

Armament comprised two or more .303 in Lewis machine-guns disposed around the car, plus one situated at the very top of the envelope, its position connected to the car by a long tube which contained a light ash ladder and which passed vertically through the envelope, a precarious station indeed. In practice it was not unusual for the upper gun to be moved down to the car itself in order to lend weight to surface target strafing, being useless for that purpose in its original position and therefore redundant unless itinerant German aircraft threatened - and in such circumstances, should the enemy be carrying incendiary ammunition, something of a token defensive gesture bearing in mind the gunner was perched on a huge, slow-moving bag of hydrogen. By mid-1916, of course, the offensive power of aircraft had grown considerably and extreme care was constantly needed to ensure the airships were kept well away from such aggressors, particularly those operating as part of the south-east and easterly regions of the RNAS network.

Sometimes, rather than being relocated to the car, the airships' upper guns were repositioned on the landing skid beneath, in which case in order to fire the weapon it was necessary to step out of the car and sit on the skid itself - a manoeuvre not for the faint-hearted, for no safety harness of any sort was employed. Generally, either four 100 or 112 lb bombs were also carried, though depth-charges or two 230 lb bombs were sometimes preferred. Even rifles were sometimes taken aloft, being used in attempts to pick off seaborne mines. A large camera could be accommodated, mounted on a simple bracket.

The parachute had been developed by the time the Mullion men took to the air, but the airship crews were not issued with such equipment. The thinking by senior military leaders of the day was that provision of such a device might encourage premature abandonment of the craft, perhaps in the face of enemy attack, by those suffering from a lack of manliness. This ridiculous 'argument' was also applied to aircraft aircrew, with the result that many hundreds died unnecessarily, particularly in combat situations, either in blazing aeroplanes they were unable to leave, or plummeting thousands of feet to an equally certain death.

The Coastal Class airship was unstable, inclined to be sluggish on the controls and its open cockpits were very uncomfortable. It was also prone to engine failures, admittedly partly a product of the formidable lengths required of its patrols. To add to those problems, difficulties were also experienced with the magnetos; pre-war, the world supplier of magnetos had been the German company Bosch, and the wartime British-built magnetos equipping the airships were much less reliable. The airship crews were obliged to become adept at changing them while in the air. The Coastal was slow, with a top speed of only 45 - 50 mph, at which, despite its reinforcing, the nose of the envelope was prone to denting. The location of the ballonet air scoop had to be moved from the original forward location to just aft of the rear engine, after it was found on operations that the original position presented an obstruction to the vision of the Coxswain. Nonetheless, despite its idiosyncrasies the C Class saw more action than any other class of British airship, and those stationed in Cornwall were amongst the busiest in the RNAS.

3 EXPANSION

Mullion's personnel quickly became numerous, not least because of the large teams essential at the beginning and end of each flight for handling and manoeuvring the airships on the ground - up to a hundred men were necessary to manhandle the Coastals in and out of the shed in unfavourable weather. In the workshops, riggers were employed in mending any punctures which developed in the envelopes of the airships, armed with rubber solution, patches and dope. They often sang while they worked, and listened for a change in pitch of voice, indicative of hydrogen inhaled from a

In the rather dingy and congested workshop within the larger shed at Mullion, fitters service the long-suffering airship engines using purpose-built benches. The area is a hive of studied industry – no doubt those present were well aware of the photographer's presence. (Author's collection)

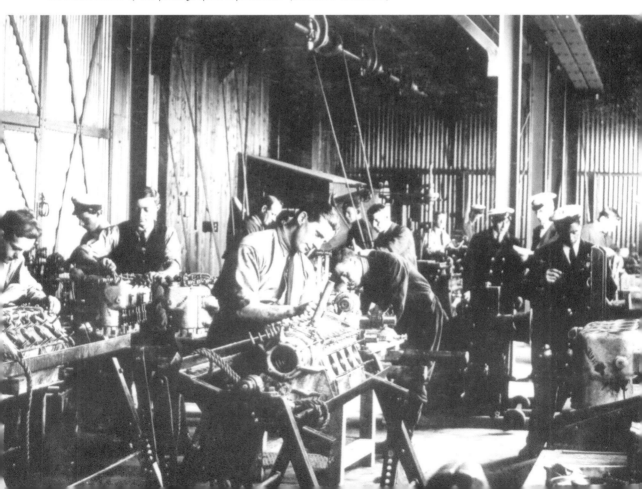

Proto gear was worn to aid the breathing of those who entered the hydrogen-filled envelopes of the airships in order to make repairs. Both riggers seen here are wearing soft shoes and the man to the left has prudently tucked his trousers in his socks to avoid catching any stray impediments. (Author's collection)

leak - although hydrogen is not poisonous, it can suffocate. Proto gear was therefore kept at Mullion, special breathing apparatus worn by those inspecting the interior of the envelopes, and originally developed for mine rescue work. The riggers also maintained the airship cables, while the fitters were kept well occupied in servicing the airships' engines between the long flights.

Mullion employed a number of Coastals during its campaign against the U-boats - C.2, C.9, C.10, C.22, and C.23a (rebuilt from the damaged C.23) all spent time there. The station's patrol areas initially stretched eastward along the Channel to Plymouth, and westward into the Atlantic beyond the Isles of Scilly. The airships quickly assumed responsibility for the air escort of convoys through the western part of the English Channel. Flights were made seven days a week, as often each day as resource and weather permitted. Over the summer of 1916 it was determined that unfortunately the north Cornish coast was not suitable for the operation of seaplanes, and from then on, the aerial patrol of the waters off that stretch was also undertaken by the Coastals. From the beginning, attempts were made to standardise the patrol patterns and shipping routes were systematically swept, while adjoining airship stations co-ordinated their efforts so as to minimise gaps and overlaps in the cover provided - a particularly important aspect of Mullion's co-operation with the similar airship base established across the Bristol Channel at Pembroke. Search patrols were often carried out in conjunction with surface vessels, notably destroyers (properly referred to at that time as torpedo boat destroyers), and trawlers armed with early forms of depth charge.

On 18 December 1916 the Admiralty established its Anti-Submarine Division under Rear-Admiral A L Duff, a step forward in co-ordinating the efforts against the U-boats. During December 1916 too, consideration was given by the Admiralty to the possibility of further airship stations for the

Coastal Class C.2 wearing bold identifying markings at Bude outstation, summer 1918. The ground handling crew share the field with a small number of cows. (Ian Stratford collection)

C*10 over the Bude outstation, autumn 1918. In the foreground is typical military tented accommodation provided for the ratings; the officers were billeted off-site. From the ground, a semaphore signal is being sent (bottom left of photograph). (RCPS Research Project)

Mullion officers with their means of transport to the surrounding villages, 1917. The vehicle wears an RN badge on its windscreen and is parked in front of the station's wardroom, which is clad with corrugated metal. A meagre lamp indicates the position of the wardroom entrance. (Author's collection)

south-west region, one to be situated at Falmouth, the other among the Isles of Scilly, on Tresco. The intended patrol areas of the new stations were to the west of the Scillies, the northern traffic route along the Channel, and northwards from Cornwall to Lundy Island. However, the plans for Falmouth did not coalesce. While some work was commenced at Tresco the station was never completed, though airships occasionally visited, making appearances over the seaplane base separately established there and mooring in the open, using a clear piece of land just to the south-east of that site.

Though the plans for airship stations at Falmouth and Tresco came to nothing, in order to allow patrols over greater areas and in an attempt to mitigate the effects upon operations of the sudden changes of local weather, a number of mooring-out stations under the control of Mullion were established. Mullion pioneered the development and use of such outstations, and the approach was later taken up by other bases. One outstation was situated a little to the south of Bude on Cornwall's far-flung north-east coast, another at Laira, a district of Plymouth, in Devon. Two further sites were established to the east along the south coast, one at Toller (Bridport, Dorset), the other at Upton (Poole, Dorset). All the outstations were commissioned over the spring and summer of 1918.

These sites were intended to be subordinate to Mullion and reported to that station in the chain of command, but their day-to-day activities were naturally reasonably autonomous because of the distances involved, though wireless allowed specific patrol patterns to be harmonised. The outstations typically accommodated one or two (but occasionally three) airships. They were equipped to carry out routine maintenance, while more complex repairs were undertaken at the central workshop in the shelter of the facilities at Mullion. The site at Laira, on the banks of the River Plym in Saltram Park, was established by a detachment of Mullion personnel, and was equipped for two Coastals, or two of the smaller, single-engined Sea Scout Zero (SSZ) Class airships. The Toller outstation was located at Gray's Farm, around a mile west of Toller Porcorum near Bridport. A

The cleared area in Bochym Wood, November 1918. Tethered in the foreground is airship SST.2, seen with its later 100,000 cu ft envelope. Behind are two SSZ Class airships, one possibly SSZ.75. A single bell tent is visible, two men at its entrance. A simple fence has been erected to discourage the surrounding trees from growing into the clearing. (J M Bruce/G S Leslie collection)

wooded area just to the north of the farm was used to provide protection for the moored airships. Officers were billeted locally, other personnel on site sharing bell-tents pitched near the farm buildings. The Upton site was situated on the Llewellin estate near Upton House, just to the north west of Poole.

RNAS Bude was designed to house two Coastals. The site was positioned some two miles south of the village of Marhamchurch, and to the south-east of Langford Woods, in a field roughly equidistant between Langford Hill and Langford Bridge. As was the case with Laira, personnel were temporarily seconded from Mullion in order to help establish Bude. A clearing was made in the adjacent wooded area, in order to provide a natural shelter from the wind for the airships. A railway line passed through nearby Bude town, and was used to bring in men, spares and provisions to the station.

While Bude's officers were quartered in comparative luxury at nearby Langford Barton House, the ratings lived in tents and a few wooden huts on site. All told, around 100 people worked at the station. The main beats carried out by Bude's airships were over the St George's and Bristol Channels, and the Irish Sea. On station the airships were kept inflated and were moored out in the open air, in the clearing within the wooded area, tied to heavy concrete balls into which were inserted iron mooring rings. For off-duty personnel, the Bullers Arms public house at Marhamchurch was one of the favoured watering-holes.

Meanwhile, Mullion had expanded its facilities locally too, occupying an area of land at nearby Bochym Wood, a modest resource with accommodation only in the form of a few bell tents, which was set in a small river valley just to the west of the Bonython Plantations. This site acted as an overspill area when the number of airships required to operate from the Lizard was too great for the main station, or at times during which the sheds at Mullion were being used for maintenance activities, and particularly when airships arriving from the outstations were receiving attention there. Again, clearings were cut in the woods, using local labour, and the surrounding trees used to provide natural shelter from the wind - like Mullion's other outstations, Bochym Wood was bereft of airship sheds. Pits were dug into the clearings, and the airships moored such that their cars sat in these, helping to improve accessibility from the ground for simple maintenance activities.

Mullion and its outstations led the way in the use of wooded areas to provide shelter for the airships in place of sheds, and as the Admiralty noted the success of the new idea, similarly sheltered sites were prepared in other parts of the country as further outstations were formed in this way. Problems of time and expense involved in erecting the huge airship sheds in out-of-the-way places could be neatly and economically circumvented, provided a combination could be found of woodland of sufficient thickness and height, coupled with a proximity to open ground which could be used to take off and land.

In addition to the dedicated airship sites, RNAS Padstow/Crugmeer, an aircraft station established on the north Cornish coast between Trevose Head and Padstow, was equipped with an airship mooring mast and received occasional visits from Mullion and Bude-based SSZ Class airships, including the SSZ.75. A mast was ideal for that station, where permanent airship residents were not envisaged. A mast crew of a few men could replace a large landing party, while an airship about to embark on patrol could simply slip its mooring in windy weather, rather than struggle to leave a shed without damaging itself in the process. The callers soon acquired the collective local epithet *The Pig*, bestowed by the civilian population - a generic name since it was difficult to tell them apart from any distance - and their bells could sometimes be heard ringing dolefully in the rolling north coast sea fogs.

4 ACTION

The C Class Mullion men, volunteers as were all RNAS airship crews, soon established that hunting the German submarines needed great reserves of tenacity in order to sustain the effectiveness of their very lengthy patrols whilst accommodated in the discomfort of the noisy and windswept open cars. It was of course necessary to provide sustenance for the crew members during the long flights, the rations for each man typically consisting of salt bacon or perhaps marmalade sandwiches, some horlicks tablets, $\frac{1}{4}$lb Cadbury's chocolate and a $\frac{1}{4}$ pint thermos of tea. On these meagre dainties men carried out operations sometimes in excess of 20 hours' duration. Very little physical movement was possible inside the car, and the crews could only stretch their legs if they were prepared to step over the side onto a thin rail which ran round the outside. Take-offs for dawn patrols were made during darkness, and night landings were sometimes carried out, usually by the light of just a few sparse lanterns, though flares were later brought into service. Because the crews were exposed to the weather for such long periods, thick flying clothes were essential; long leather coats, heavy boots and gauntlets were typical items worn and over time, attire assumed an interesting informality as individuals dressed in the warmest ways they could. Despite these measures, however, on return to base the aviators had sometimes to be lifted from the gondolas by

kindly ground crew, their limbs stiff and frozen from the wind and cold.

Although the Admiralty may have felt some degree of optimism regarding the power of aerial observation compared with attempts at sea level, sighting the submarines in fact proved extremely difficult. During favourable weather, over calm seas uncluttered by white-caps, the wake (or 'feather') of a periscope or the shadow of the enemy travelling just below the surface might sometimes be detected. The U-boats also tended to leak oil from their periscopes, propellers, rudders and hydroplane bearings, though such emissions were usually faint unless damage had been sustained to those areas. The wake of a discharged torpedo could also provide an indicator. The painstaking searches for these signs by the airship crews demanded fierce concentration on the surface of the sea for hours on end, and disappointingly, many objects which at first sight appeared to indicate the presence of a submarine turned out on closer examination to be merely floating detritus. Usually a surfaced submarine would see the approaching airship first, of course, which made the job of catching the enemy unawares doubly difficult.

Stephen Henry Bromhead flew in Short 184s from Newlyn, then transferred to airships, serving on C.9 and later the SSZ class. Here he displays typical aircrew clothing in the form of a heavy leather greatcoat, thick trousers and warm boots. A leather flying helmet would have been worn in the air. (Ian Stratford collection)

Flight Lieutenant Struthers sits on the edge of C.9's cockpit. He is not wearing flying kit and the engine of the airship is stopped, suggesting that perhaps this is a posed photo taken at ground level. Struthers' RNAS cuff insignia, two gold bands surmounted by a gold eagle, is visible. The attachment points of the car to the envelope can be clearly made out. (Ian Stratford collection)

The second of Mullion's sheds under construction, mid 1917. The scale of the structures can be seen from the personnel working by the main doors, and from the figure standing by the trusses for the wind breaks. (Author's collection)

A further possibility, however, was the psychological one. The airship crews noted that, having fired a torpedo at a ship it was sometimes impossible for the U-boat captain to resist surfacing, in order to learn whether his strike had been successful. By circling over the scene of the action until the enemy assumed the coast was clear and rose, the opportunity might arise for the airship to launch its own attack.

Notwithstanding the offensive capability of the airships, the real strength of the patrols was their deterrent value. The key to the campaign, perhaps easier to recognise with hindsight than at the time, was that what mattered most was an uninterrupted flow of merchant shipping; the sinking of U-boats was not a necessity as long as they were discouraged from attacking the vital supply lanes. Indeed, the fear of detection from above succeeded in creating a level of caution among the submarines in surfacing to recharge their batteries; this in turn could make them much less effective, blunting their ability to move rapidly. While on the surface, the sight of an approaching airship would usually be enough to make a U-boat submerge smartly - though occasionally the commander would decide to remain afloat and fight it out with his aerial tormentor using his deck weaponry. It was quite out of the question for the Germans to provide any air cover for U-boats operating in the western part of the Channel, let alone in the Atlantic, for the range of their aircraft was not adequate, so Mullion's airships could patrol without fear of such opposition. In practice therefore, in addition to attacks on the U-boats the machine-guns fitted to the Cornish Coastals were often used for strafing surface targets such as mines, and wreckage judged dangerous to shipping with the purpose of sinking it.

Two important factors which fundamentally affected the strategic operational control of the airships were the use of wireless direction-finding (DF) and telegraphy equipment. A DF station was erected at Mullion and another at Prawle Point in south-west Devon, and these bases took regular cross-bearings of the patrols operating in the south-western approaches, using the call-signs transmitted every hour by the airships. This enabled the position of each airship to be determined accurately, even when it was out of sight of land, though of course unfortunately the transmissions were in turn susceptible to German interception.

Wireless telegraphy (W/T) communications between the airships and their base was another innovation introduced when a W/T station was established on the Lizard, though the equipment sometimes developed faults. When this happened messages had to be routed via a third party, often Devonport itself, or delivered to Mullion by motor car from the Lizard when the local telephone line was not working, a journey of about fifteen minutes on the roads of the day. Using the wireless, the Senior Naval Officers at Falmouth and Penzance could be kept abreast of the defenders' aerial

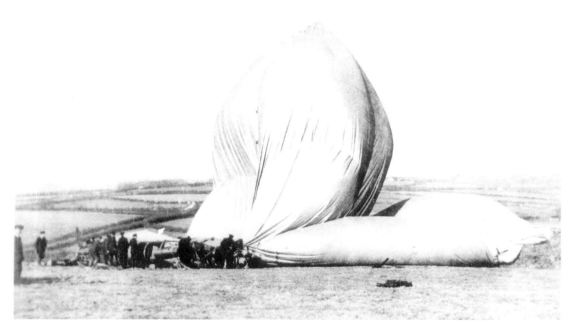

Coastal airship C.6 was based at the RNAS station at Pembroke but crash-landed near Mullion on 2 December 1916. Fortunately there were no casualties. The envelope is being deflated preparatory to recovering the craft in order to assess the damage. The car of the airship is to the left of the collapsed envelope. (Ces Mowthorpe collection)

C.9 on patrol over a placid English Channel during 1918, wearing her identity on the lower forward area of her envelope. Her ballonet air scoop arrangement has been modified. In the background is the southern Cornish coastline. (J M Bruce/G S Leslie collection)

activities, while patrols carried out between destroyers and airships or aircraft benefited from the RNAS employing the same W/T wavelength as the destroyers in order to provide rapid communication.

Further progress was made with the establishment of an Intelligence Office at Mullion during the latter part of 1917, which was responsible for co-ordinating information on the habits of enemy submarines in general, and for plotting in particular all that was learned of U-boat activities in the locality. By collecting and analysing various types of information, it became possible to predict the future areas of U-boat operations with a greater degree of confidence than hitherto, and thereby plan the routes of airship patrols with more precision. Particular attention was paid to information on the type of submarines encountered by the aerial and surface defenders, their last reported positions, the weather conditions at the time, and the plotted tracks of other submarines in the area. Also considered was the enemy's general method of working, including resting times and places, and times at which the submarines were most active. An assessment was then made of the best protection that could be provided to shipping, having in view the trade routes, and patrols were set both for the protection of shipping and for the destruction of submarines. Meanwhile, the positions of patrolling airships, collected by the DF stations, was also fed to the Intelligence Office, where they were plotted on a chart. Should an encounter with the enemy be reported, the nearest airship and surface vessels could be diverted to the scene. This rapidly transmitted and reasonably accurate information played an important part in providing the wherewithal to help counter the U-boats. Following the success of the Mullion office, intelligence centres were established in other regions.

Off-duty, Mullion's isolation made for a quiet life, the local inns providing a diversion while the scenery made for good walking when the weather was fine. The rare flora and fauna of the Lizard, as well as its unusual geology provided points of interest, and the nearest small town, Helston, was a popular visit where essentials could be obtained. Once the initial reticence of the surrounding farmers over the establishment of the base was overcome, they would often donate home-grown produce to the personnel there. This was a real measure of their regard for the Mullion men, because food was ever more scarce, and as the war ran on the situation grew acute even in rural areas. Over the period of the RNAS tenure, several servicemen met and married local girls.

During the patrols, meanwhile, the airships would sometimes liaise with the lighthouses surrounding Cornwall's coast. In particular, the Wolf Rock lighthouse had its newspapers delivered by airship from time to time, and in return kept literally a weather eye out for mines and submarines. In the time permitting between their patrol duties, the airship flight crews conducted various practice exercises, particularly bombing sorties using dummy bombs dropped on targets set out within the station boundary but away from the centres of activity. Experiments with flag signalling apparatus and later with airborne hydrophone equipment,
were also carried out by Mullion crews.

*

Of the airships based in Cornwall the most famous was Mullion's Coastal Class 9, which was sometimes referred to as the 'darling of the airship service'. C.9 was involved in many incidents and adventures during an outstanding career, destroying one U-boat for certain and responsible for the possible demise of at least three others, a remarkable feat especially considering its limited offensive capability and its role which was intended to be primarily reconnaissance - the airships were expected to rely on the co-operation and hitting power of surface vessels and aircraft in pressing home the attacks. Indeed, C.9 probably held the finest operational record of any RNAS airship throughout the war.

C.9 was captained initially by Flight Lieutenant J G Struthers. She arrived at Mullion by rail on 15 June and performed her first flight there on 1 July, which lasted $1\frac{1}{2}$ hours. She endured a harrowing episode shortly after this, on Sunday 22 July, when after 19 hours and some 520 miles on patrol (at that time a record for endurance of the type), both engines became unserviceable off the Channel Islands. The destroyer HMS *Foyle* took the airship in tow but during the return to Mullion the envelope of C.9 gradually lost pressure and buckled; the crew were obliged to transfer to the ship. The shelter of Mullion cove was eventually reached despite this situation, where the airship finally came down in the water. Following a brief period lashed to the smaller quay at Mullion harbour, C.9 was transported back to her station by road for repair.

On examination, both the envelope and the car were found to have received bullet holes, momentos of C.9's time over Jersey that day, where the (British) ground troops had evidently been unable to distinguish between friend and foe despite having been advised of her impending call, and the fact that she was carrying national markings. However, repairs were quickly effected and C.9 was soon back in harness; by the end of the year she had completed $177\frac{1}{2}$ hours of operational flying.

On 2 December 1916, the local inhabitants had a shock when airship C.6, from the RNAS station at Pembroke, force-landed near Mullion. A recovery team was despatched from the station and succeeded in resuscitating the airship, which was put back into service, though it was lost at sea during March of the following year due to engine trouble.

Early during the following February meanwhile, on patrol in C.9 off the Lizard, Struthers spied what appeared to be the underwater path of a U-boat. He located a small group of trawlers nearby and advised them, by Aldis lamp, of the enemy below. His warnings complete, he then took more robust action, dropping a bomb at the head of the path. Though there was no indication of success at the

C.9, moored in Mullion's small harbour during July 1916 following her partial deflation care of bullets received over Jersey from British troops, who struck despite the obvious national markings carried by the airship. The rearmost portion of the car trails in the water. RNAS personnel populate the pier while local people watch from the bank above the harbour. (RCPS Research Project)

time of the action, the trawlers subsequently recovered some wreckage (though it was not clearly U-boat material) while the submarine was not sighted again. This episode resulted in a claim for a possible sinking, albeit a rather hopeful one.

Struthers made a further attack during the late morning of 12 February whilst proceeding on a course due north from the Wolf Rock, on a submarine detected seven miles north-west of Cape Cornwall. The position of the U-boat was betrayed to the airship by a suspicious track of what appeared to be oil and bubbles. C.9 descended from some 1,600 ft to around 400 ft, and at the lower altitude was able to confirm the track was indeed caused by a submarine, travelling in a south-west direction at around ten knots. The airship attacked in consort with three armed trawlers (FD836 and two others) which she had managed to attract by daylight flash-lamp. A 65 lb bomb was released just ahead of the track, at an airspeed of 15 kts. The delivery of the bomb onto the trail head was in line with the predicted path of the U-boat. C.9 remained on observation over the spot for nearly three hours but the sure signs of damage or destruction, excessive oil and air bubble discharge, were not reported. After a further search of over two hours, the airship continued her patrol eastwards to Trevose Head. The trawlers stayed to comb the area with their sweeps deployed, however, and the sweeps of one exploded some 300 yards to the south-west of the spot where the bomb had been dropped. A certain amount of wreckage was subsequently found, which it was thought may have come from the enemy.

On 22 February C.9 escorted eight Dutch steamers from Falmouth west toward the Isles of Scilly. A short distance from their destination the airship bade farewell to its charges but the

U-21 (*Kapitänleutnant* Hersing), returning to base from a patrol in the Adriatic, had been stalking the convoy and at just after 5 pm commenced an attack, sinking six of the eight vessels, a bitter lesson in perseverance for the RNAS.

Also during that eventful month, Struthers observed a wreck off the Lizard which was creating a potential danger to shipping, and requested it be sunk by surface vessel gunfire. He was ordered by wireless to return to Mullion but refused, preferring to stay in the vicinity for some nine hours until a destroyer arrived, so he could see for himself the danger had been dealt with. The length of time taken before the destroyer appeared was due to an initially incorrect D/F reading of the incident which had placed the location in the middle of Dartmoor. Upon returning to Mullion, instead of receiving a reprimand the crew of C.9 were congratulated on their perseverance.

In February 1917 too, the erection was commenced of a second airship shed at Mullion, which had been moved there from the station at Dover. This shed was smaller and of more prefabricated construction than the first, with wooden frames and corrugated iron cladding, and was suitable for just a single airship. The increase in activity around the areas patrolled by Mullion's airships had made it essential to add to the resource in that region.

15 March witnessed an extremely dangerous situation which developed aboard C.9 while the airship was escorting merchant vessels near Plymouth. The aft engine caught fire and flames began to lick toward the hydrogen-filled envelope. The engineer aboard, Air Mechanic Parkes, promptly sat astride the offending engine casing, dousing himself and the surrounding area with the contents of a fire extinguisher, a drastic action in order to avoid certain disaster. C.9 limped back to Mullion on its forward engine, and on subsequent examination it was discovered the rear airscrew mounting bolts had sheared; the resulting friction of the airscrew about the shaft had caused the fire. Air Mechanic Parkes appears to have received no official recognition of his bravery and, his trousers ruined, was obliged to purchase another pair from his own money, which seems rather harsh under the circumstances!

On 3 April 1917, a new development emerged which affected the campaign in the south-west, when Wing Commander Eugene L Gerrard was appointed on the staff of C in C HM Ships and Vessels Devonport, to take command of the air stations at Cattewater (Plymouth), Scilly, Newlyn and Fishguard, and the airship bases at Mullion and Pembroke. Gerrard was a very experienced officer whose background was with the Royal Marines Light Infantry, and who previously had led No 1 Squadron RNAS, No 2 Squadron RNAS and later 2 Group RNAS; back in 1911 he had flown the very first aircraft to bear a serial of that service (or at least, that of the then Naval Wing of the Royal Flying Corps), a Short Pusher biplane unimaginatively numbered '1'. The new command was designated the South Western Group with its Headquarters at Mount Wise, Devonport, and replaced the structure originally established under the Anti-Submarine Division. Two similar Groups were also created to administer other areas of the country.

A more strategic reorganisation commenced shortly after the formation of the South Western Group. On 28 April, following considerable deliberation on the effectiveness or otherwise of the convoy philosophy in affording protection for merchant vessels, the Admiralty informed Gibraltar's Senior Naval Officer convoys would be introduced from that port, on a trial basis. Accordingly, on the evening of 10 May the first such convoy, comprising sixteen merchant ships, set sail for England. These vessels were escorted by two armed merchantmen and three armed yachts. Eight days later, merchantmen and escorts arrived safely off the British coast, where they were greeted by six destroyers from Devonport - and significantly from the point of view of the westernmost RNAS presence, an H.12 twin-engined maritime patrol flying-boat from the station on Tresco. The success of the experiment was most encouraging and over the next few weeks convoys were introduced more widely. Falmouth became an assembly port for convoys outbound to Gibraltar and Dakar, Plymouth for convoys to the Atlantic ports.

That April also witnessed another inconclusive action by C.9 on a suspected submarine while two months later, on 22 June, a destroyer spotted a U-boat some 15 miles south of Start Point and the nearby airship arrived to drop a 65 lb delayed action bomb, to which the destroyer added two depth charges. Following the latter action, German radio broadcasts were monitored by Mullion's wireless station and it was noted that calls made to the U-boat from its base went unanswered.

Early on the morning of 9 August, a convoy including the USS *Cleveland* was escorted by a mixed bag of aerial allies in a combined operation which became typical of the area. A Tresco-based H.12 made contact with the vessels at around 5.30 am, shepherding them as far as Mount's Bay when a Short 184 from Newlyn took over. As the convoy proceeded further east, Coastal C.2 accompanied by SSZ Class airship Number 14 appeared from Mullion, relieving the seaplane, taking up positions on the starboard and port bows respectively. After around an hour and a half, both airships spotted a U-boat travelling northward on course to intercept the convoy, at some seven miles distant. The two immediately closed with the enemy, dropping two 100 lb bombs at the submarine as it submerged. A search was then conducted, assisted by a Short 184 from Newlyn, while two British and two American destroyers depth-charged the area. In addition, Sopwith 1½ Strutters made three flights over the vicinity while the two airships remained for several hours, but the submarine was not located. However, it was felt some damage may have been inflicted, and the presence of the RNAS assisted in keeping the U-boat at bay while the convoy reached Falmouth safely.

On 13 August 1917, Flight Lieutenant Struthers was mentioned in despatches for his attacks and escort work, and for having flown well over 1,000 hours on patrol. During the early morning of 17 August, C.9 was patrolling the area around the Eddystone lighthouse when an upturned hull was spotted. This was the wreck of the 2,500 ton SS *Claverley*, out of Newcastle, which had been torpedoed at 2.00 am that morning. Amongst the wreckage two lifeboats were also observed, one occupied by five men of whom three were still alive, while a further man was seen floating in the water with the aid of a lifebelt. C.9 was able to report the sighting with the signal, 'Large capsized steamer. Men alive in waterlogged lifeboat. Remaining over till marked. Assistance at once'. The airship then hailed the survivors to inform them help was on the way, and attracted the attention of some nearby trawlers. A number of fortunate survivors were picked up, being subsequently landed at Plymouth. The *Claverley* was then sunk by gunfire from one of the trawlers in order to prevent her becoming a danger to other shipping.

During an afternoon in September, C.9 was searching for mines when she encountered the oil tanker *San Dustano*, which had been torpedoed earlier, part of a convoy bound for Falmouth. The airship accompanied the steamers toward the safety of Falmouth harbour, sweeping ahead and abeam of the convoy, in consort with four tugs and eight trawlers. However, a U-boat was suddenly sighted on the surface some ten miles astern of the convoy on the starboard quarter. Struthers gave chase, though the submarine rapidly submerged, and released two 100 lb bombs, 100 ft ahead and 250 ft ahead of its predicted course. Violent explosions took place and a large patch of oil came to the surface. A seaplane (almost certainly a Short 184 from Newlyn) and an armed trawler arrived to assist in the attack and at 6.30 pm a fierce explosion resulted from below. No more was seen of the submarine and the convoy made Falmouth safely. C.9 finally returned to Mullion at 8.30 pm.

On 21 September C.9 was on early patrol off the Lizard, having left Mullion at 5 am, when the French steamer *Rouang* was sighted some ten miles south of the Lizard, escorted by a trawler, having been torpedoed within the previous half hour. A rigorous search was immediately commenced and some five hours later a U-boat was detected, on the surface 15 miles south-east of The Lizard, heading north-east and thought to be intending an attack on a convoy bound for Falmouth. C.9 at once gave chase. As the U-boat observed him and began to crash-dive, Struthers dropped two delayed action 100 lb bombs some 300 ft in front of the final swirl of the periscope. This immediately resulted in a violent explosion which brought large bubbles of air and oil to the surface. However, after waiting for signs confirming the destruction of the U-boat, at 1.30 pm Struthers was obliged to return to Mullion for fuel, and also took the opportunity to load more bombs; replacement airships C.2 and C.23a continued to reconnoitre assisted by the destroyer HMS *Laverock* and the auxiliary minesweeper *Fusilier*, which had arrived shortly after mid-day.

When he returned to the scene at 5.00 pm Struthers found an oil slick covering almost a square mile of sea, its position fixed as 16 miles south-south-east of the Lizard. *Laverock* swept the area with her paravanes until 6.30 pm without result, but noted the presence of a refined type of oil such as petrol or paraffin on the surface of the water. The following day a trawler at the spot momentarily recovered a piece of steel plate in its nets (though unfortunately it was dropped before it could be brought aboard) and it became clear the submarine had indeed been destroyed by C.9, one of the very few airships to have sunk a U-boat without any assistance from surface craft.

Patrolling between the Lizard and Eddystone on 29 September, Struthers sighted and attacked a submarine to the east of the Eddystone lighthouse. Moving easterly at around five knots, the U-boat had disturbed the lower water containing mud and sediment, and the trail marking its passage, some two miles in length, was visible from the air. After releasing a calcium flare to mark the spot, Struthers called up two armed trawlers. C.9 then dropped a 100 lb bomb at the head of the trail, and the trawler CV 567 two depth charges, which resulted in the appearance of an oily track and air bubbles. Further depth-charges were released by the trawler at the head of the track, following which a much greater discharge of oil and bubbles appeared, that time from a source which was clearly stationary. The spot was marked by a buoy while the trawler CV 34 went for more depth charges, returning in the late afternoon together with two further trawlers and a torpedo boat destroyer. Two more depth charges were released at the spot, and oil continued to rise to the surface. It was agreed the U-boat had probably been destroyed. At 4.30 pm Struthers returned to Mullion, low on fuel, after a patrol lasting 11 hours.

On 2 October Struthers was awarded the DSC. Two days later C.9 was between Eddystone and the Lizard escorting a west-bound convoy accompanied by the usual complement of torpedo boat destroyers. C23a, also from Mullion, arrived over the scene and took over that escort from C.9, the latter signalling her sister-ship 'Working SW with one large mine-layer and four torpedo boat destroyers from Eddystone'. Struthers then observed a second convoy, together with one *Carnarvon* Class cruiser and two torpedo boat destroyers, over which C.9 kept watch for a time. Inside Eddystone the airship prepared to hand her charges over to the airship SSZ.15, which had also arrived from Mullion. Just as Struthers was about to leave the ships, believing them safe, a huge spout of water was sighted; one of the merchant ships had been torpedoed.

Struthers at once raced toward the damaged vessel, achieving a speed of some 85 mph thanks to a strong tailwind of well over 30 mph; he arrived at the scene so swiftly the track of the U-boat's torpedo was still visible, running at right-angles to the direction of the convoy. The airship crew were able to observe the shadow of the submarine, some 20 - 40 ft below the surface and moving slowly westward. Struthers released two 100 lb bombs at the target, which fell right on top of it, and immediately there was a great detonation from below. Air bubbles and oil rose to the surface and the trawlers *Derby* and *Stanley Weyman* arrived to release depth charges on a calcium flare dropped from the airship, which itself added two more 100 lb bombs. This brought forth more air bubbles; the signs were that the U-boat had been at least badly damaged. In the meantime, a steamer had arrived beneath the cover of the airship, and was successful in rescuing the survivors of the torpedoed vessel, which had sunk fifteen minutes after having been struck. As the surface vessels moved away from the scene, C.9 commenced a grim struggle back to Mullion in the face of the powerful wind, a forty-mile journey which took six hours to complete.

In indifferent weather during early December 1917, Struthers attacked yet another U-boat, that time at a position some 100 miles south-west of the Isles of Scilly and some 120 miles away from his station. The airship crew had sighted a thin line of oil, and after careful study decided it was moving and extending, though no submarine was visible to them. The airship released a speculative 230 lb bomb 100 ft in front of what was thought to be the path of the U-boat. A huge explosion promptly occurred, sufficient to seriously disturb the airship flying at around 1,000 ft, and forward movement of the track ceased. A small amount of air and oil came to the surface, and Struthers waited patiently for the enemy to surface. However, C.9 was obliged to leave the scene, being unable to remain looking for signs confirming her success because of the deteriorating weather, and arriving back at Mullion in heavy rain.

Struthers was awarded two bars to his DSC on 11 December and six days later relinquished command of C.9, leaving for Longside, Angus, and command of the North Sea Class NS.6 airship there, a larger type of craft than the Coastal series, employing a crew of ten. Flight Lieutenant T P York-Moore assumed command of C.9 as the patrols from Cornwall continued unabated.

During Boxing Day 1917, an unfortunate and very rare gap in the British airship U-boat defences was revealed. As a convoy formed up outside Falmouth harbour, bound for Gibraltar, two ships were torpedoed even though the airships were on duty above. Despite a quickly organised search, their assailant succeeded in escaping the vengeful defenders.

1917 saw C.9 complete 1,042 hours 42 minutes of operational flying. On 9 April 1918 she escorted the damaged SS *Tainui* to Falmouth, a journey made slow and potentially dangerous as the ship was in tow, having been damaged by a torpedo the previous day. She was finally deflated on 14 September 1918 for an inspection, and was formally struck off charge as beyond any further repair on 1 October, having flown a total of 3,720 hours and an estimated 68,200 miles, more than any other airship in the Service. In her operational life of 805 days it was claimed she had never been unavailable for patrols because of unserviceability. By contrast, C.10 had lasted less than four months, being delivered to Mullion on 19 June 1916, again by rail, and being deleted following an accident there on 10 October.

*

In terms of attacks against U-boats, although the crew of C.9 were very much in the front line they did not monopolise events; other Mullion Coastals also had their day. During 9 September 1916 C.10 was patrolling off The Lizard accompanied on the surface by the destroyer *Foyle*, when two burning ships were sighted. The airship quickly went to investigate and a U-boat was spotted on the far side of the ships, but dived while C.10 was still several hundred yards away. A strong wind was breaking the surface of the water, which made it difficult to distinguish the U-boat's trail, but bombs were released at the head of its estimated path. A careful search made by the airship and the *Foyle* revealed no indication of a successful strike. In fact the U-boat had survived and resurfaced some time later, perhaps drawn by curiosity, but an attack from the *Foyle* caused it promptly to disappear once more, and no further siting was made.

Though the latter attack too was inconclusive, the submarine had at least been driven off. This episode in fact marked the first attack by an RNAS airship on a U-boat. The burning vessels turned out to be French sailing ships which the submarine had strafed with gunfire while surfaced. The U-boat captain had then compelled the French crews to transfer provisions to his submarine. The transfer had been underway when the Germans had sighted the airship and (perhaps understandably) had panicked; in their haste to dive, they had abandoned a quantity of stores taken from the Frenchmen which had been assembled on the U-boat's decking. Some of the items survived their ordeal and were recovered (including the Panama hat belonging to one of the French skippers), being put aboard the *Foyle*, which had also picked up the survivors of the action.

12 February 1917 was indeed an active day in the life of Mullion. Earlier during the same day as C.9 would engage a submarine off Cape Cornwall, the C.22, commanded by Flight Sub-Lieutenant C S Coltson, observed a Norwegian steamer with lowered boats, together with the wreck of a second ship, around 10 miles ESE of Falmouth. Two trawlers (436 *John C Meikle* and 1995 *Gavina*) quickly arrived at the scene and descending to 200 ft, Coltson learned the ship had been torpedoed. He at once commenced a search for the U-boat, hoping it had remained in the vicinity. Surprisingly, the imprudent submarine was found surfaced only a short distance way, moving in a westerly direction, but as Coltson moved at full speed to deliver his attack he was spotted and the enemy started to dive. From 1,000 ft Coltson released one bomb, which landed a little ahead of the path; unfortunately it failed to explode. His airship, its helm hard over, released a second bomb almost at once, at the point where the submarine had submerged, with evidently more successful results for that time a considerable quantity of oil rose to the surface. The trawlers swept the area and the sweep of the *Gavina* was almost immediately exploded, but nothing came to the surface, C.22 remained in the vicinity for four hours following the attack but no sign was seen of the U-boat, which Coltson felt had been sunk by the second bomb. After both engines developed faults the airship was reluctantly obliged to return home, landing at Mullion just after 3.00 pm in poor visibility and drizzle.

On 9 March 1917 another attack was made, that time on a surfaced U-boat moving in the direction of a convoy sailing off the Lizard. C.22 dropped her entire bombload, and the accompanying trawlers their depth charges. Though the submarine wisely dived, a success was assumed after a great oil slick appeared on the surface. However, C.22 was lost on 21 March, midway between Ushant and Land's End, though happily her crew of four were rescued.

A further action took place on 9 August 1917 as C.2 was escorting a convoy through the Western Approaches. A surfaced U-boat was spotted some seven miles distant with the obvious intention of intercepting the convoy. The submarine remained surfaced until the airship was only two miles away, but then promptly submerged. C.2 dropped two 100 lb bombs two minutes after the conning tower had disappeared, 200 and 300 yards ahead of the predicted course of the U-boat, and this produced the emergence of a small amount of oil. Four destroyers arrived to join in the search and a large quantity of oil was subsequently spotted on the surface. No further move was made by the submarine and the convoy passed safely. Indeed, no submarine was reported in the area over the next six days.

Coastal C.23a also made a contribution. Arriving for service at Mullion on 4 September 1917 from Folkestone, during the early afternoon of 17 November 1917 she was off Dodman Point under the command of Flight Lieutenant R L Montagu, when a large amount of wreckage, with a trawler and a steamer standing by, were observed. From the two craft Montagu learned the wreckage was the former SS *Victoria*, which had been torpedoed only a few minutes earlier. Patrolling the vicinity, Montagu observed what appeared to be a submarine about twenty feet beneath the surface, making three to four knots. Climbing to 800 ft, the airship overflew the head of the trail and dropped two 100 lb bombs, the explosions of which were followed by the emergence of air bubbles to the water's surface. The trawler *Flintshire*, meanwhile, having witnessed the attack, made for the position at full speed and let go a depth charge which brought a quantity of wood to the surface.

The airship then dropped calcium flares to mark the position of the action and, when these floated away, further indicated the spot to the trawler, using Lewis gun fire. More depth charges were released and the trawler's port and starboard towed charges were fired in the neighbourhood of the flares. C.23a then signalled the trawler to buoy the position, by which time oil was rising, while the pilot, coming down close to the water, spoke to the skipper, ordering that further buoys be placed in positions he would indicate. These orders were carried out and shortly afterwards, ML.331 arrived on the scene, straddling the patch with two further charges. The airship remained until darkness fell, eventually returning to Mullion after 9¾ hours. Though it was never confirmed the submarine was sunk by the attack, there seemed clear evidence to suggest it was damaged. However, in sharp counterpoint to that action, just before midnight during the same day the SS *Arabis* was torpedoed within a few miles of the previous events; the thinking at the time was that her assailant was the submarine attacked earlier in the day.

C.23a served from September 1917 until May 1918, when she was lost in very unusual circumstances. On 10 May she was patrolling the north Cornish coast travelling north-east along the shoreline toward Newquay, around one mile offshore at an altitude of some 400 ft. While passing over the mid-point of Crantock Bay suddenly a U-boat surfaced, from which the crew quickly took up position with their powerful deck gun. Before horrified eye-witnesses on shore, the Germans succeeded in shooting down C.23a. The airship broke in two and fell into the bay. Her pilot, Captain A J Elliott, and the engineer were saved but the W/T Operator was drowned - there is no record of other crew members. The wreckage of the airship was recovered and towed into Newquay harbour where it was made secure against the South Quay; subsequently it was moved to Pembroke, where perhaps some items were used as spares - the airship itself was deleted from the strength of the RNAS at that time.

5 THE SSZ CLASS

In addition to the C Class, Mullion and its out-stations also operated the smaller Submarine Scout Zero (SSZ) Class airships: Numbers 14, 15, 25, 27, 40, 42, 45, 47, 49 and 75 served there. The SSZ employed an envelope of 143 ft in length, with a volume of 70,000 cu ft and containing two ballonets. It was powered by a single engine, a 75 hp Rolls-Royce Hawk pusher designed from the outset specifically to power that particular class of airship. The aluminium and ash car of the SSZ accommodated three and was of much improved design over that of the C Class, having a boat-like profile which provided a degree of crew comfort and also allowed the airship to alight on the water if necessary. The complement consisted of the W/T operator in the forward position, the pilot in the central position and aft of him, adjacent to the powerplant, the engineer. Armament comprised two 110 lb bombs or one 230/250 lb bomb, together with a single Lewis machine-gun in the forward position. The first production SSZs appeared during June 1917 and eventually 77 were commissioned.

Mullion in mature configuration, summer 1917. The second shed is erected and its screening is almost complete. The scars of the building work have faded and four Sopwith 1½ Strutters are positioned near the single Bessoneau hangar - further such hangars were added subsequently. The number of buildings has grown considerably, especially at the northern end of the site (top left of photograph). The photo was taken on a sunny afternoon. (Author's collection)

As with the C Class the strength of the SSZs was their deterrent value. Many long patrols were flown but few incidents against the U-boats were recorded. Generally, events seem to have been centred around mechanical failures and accidents rather than successful offensive actions, which would be consistent with the primarily reconnaissance role of the SSZ airships, combined with the great lengths demanded of their patrols. For example, SSZ.14, used for landing trials at Tresco during August 1917, suffered engine failure on 7 September of that year after leaving Mullion on a morning patrol at just after 9.00 am, under the command of Flight Lieutenant Elliott (later Captain Elliott, who would be shot down off Newquay in C.23a). Flying over the Channel, late that afternoon the usually reliable Hawk broke down. SSZ.14 signalled her position and rose to some 2,500 ft, drifting south-south-westerly. An hour later the airship's drogue was lost but an efficient substitute was improvised from coats, seats and petrol cans. However, to add to the problems of the crew, the craft began to sink uncontrollably and it became necessary to jettison much loose equipment, including the Lewis gun.

Fortunately, at 5.45 pm the sun came out, which caused the phenomenon known as 'superheating', the hydrogen in the airship's envelope reacting to the increase in temperature rather more quickly

Above the English Channel, SSZ.42 keeps a vigilant watch over a lone vessel during the latter half of 1918. By that time, she bore her identity on her envelope. (Author's collection)

Spring 1918. Flight Lieutenants Montagu and Yorke-Moore (seated at front) with C.9's team in front of the main doors of Mullion's larger airship shed. Because of their considerable weight, the doors were located on rail-mounted running-gear, which can be seen here. (Author's collection)

Left. SSZ.42 at Bude during the latter half of 1918. Its engine is running, and a small handling party holds one guy rope. (Ian Stratford collection)

SSZ.42, with pennants flying, low over Mullion's northern side. Her mechanic stands in the rear of the car to attend to the engine. In the background is some of the hutted accommodation erected at the site, in which curtains are visible. (Helston Folk Museum)

than does air, resulting in a short period of 'false' lift. Because of this, the SSZ.14 was able to make height once more, rising to an altitude of around 3,500 ft. However, all attempts to start the engine failed, though the home-made drogue worked well to keep the airship shearing just off the wind, and by 6.30 pm she was 40 miles south of Start Point, Devon, and drifting south.

Further items were jettisoned as the craft began to sink again; the ammunition tray, revolvers and pyrenes, the cartridges and cover for the Aldis lamp, the oil from the oil tank, water from the radiator, even the explosive from the bombs - though apparently, not the bombs themselves. SSZ.14 managed to stagger to the French coast and at 9.15 pm finally managed to alight safely

Bude outstation, summer 1918: the car of SSZ.42 with quite a mixture of people in attendance, among them RNAS and Army-uniformed personnel. The Lewis gun mount is visible by the forward cockpit. (Ian Stratford collection)

The car of SSZ.25 in the shed at Mullion, between December 1917 and January 1918. The bomb installations, mounting 110 lb bombs, are visible, as is the machine-gun, which fires forward. Amidships, a large camera is installed. Behind the car, the fin of an airship has been stored. (J M Bruce/G S Leslie collection).

at St Jean du Doight, Finisterre, having free ballooned for some 120 miles. The crew emerged unscathed from their flight and managed to deflate the envelope before any further damage was caused. The airship was then taken by wagon to the French airship station at Guipavas. The engine was subsequently repaired and two weeks later, on 21 September, the refitted SSZ.14 made the return trip to Mullion, airship and crew none the worse for their ordeal. She lost her envelope in a storm at Laira on 20 January 1918, and on 6 November that year crashed into a tree during darkness and was deflated during the following day, never, it seems, flying again.

Of the other Cornish SSZs, SSZ.25 broke loose from its moorings and was wrecked in a gale at Laira during January 1918 while SSZ.15 was lost at sea two miles south of Exmouth during the following April while operating from Toller. SSZ.45 crashed at Toller Down, around three miles north of the local mooring-out station in July 1918, but was put back into service, experiencing a second forced-landing near Radipole on 15 August. SSZ.49 was lost at sea on 2 September 1918. SSZ.40 suffered a crash-landing at Leedstown, near Camborne, on 21 December, but was not struck off charge until October 1919. Meanwhile SSZ.42 was used on at least one humanitarian mission when its W/T Operator, Stephen Henry Bromhead, (who previously had served with Struthers on C.9 and had flown in Short 184 seaplanes from Newlyn) dropped a message contained in a matchbox into the garden of his sweetheart's house at Marhamchurch to inform her he would be late for their date, after the airship had been unexpectedly called on patrol from nearby Bude.

The car of M.T.1 at Mullion during early 1918. The location of the Hawk engines on gantries adjoining the car must have made for extremely noisy accommodation. However, the pilot was unlikely to have been distracted from his labours by the complexity of the instrumentation! (Kind permission RNAS Culdrose)

6 MULLION'S OWN AIRSHIP

During the early part of 1918 a new and experimental class of airship appeared, designed at RNAS Mullion by a group of officers led by Flight Lieutenant R L.Montagu and stemming from the SSZ Class. The Mullion officers had reservations over operating the SSZs - despite the high regard in which the Rolls Royce Hawk was held, its singularity was considered a risk when flying over water for long periods. In order to overcome the problem, the officers developed the so-called *Mullion Twin*. The new airship, originally designated the M.T.1, became redesignated the SSE.2 ('E' for Experimental) during the summer of 1918. It also acquired the rather effusive local epithet *Silver Queen*, though that was not the first time such a title had been used - His Majesty's Airship No 4, delivered in 1913 to the Royal Aircraft Factory at Farnborough from the German Parseval Airship Company, had also borne that unofficial name.

The SSE.2 was powered by two 75 hp Rolls Royce Hawk engines located one each side of the car, mounted on gantries and driving pusher propellers. The car provided accommodation for a crew of four or five; one or two pilots, W/T operator, coxswain and engineer. Originally fitted with an 85,000 cu ft envelope, this capacity was subsequently increased to 100,000 cu ft. The new airship was delivered in March 1918. Its first trial flight was made on 4 March and lasted just over one hour during which the craft achieved 55 knots, but on 15 March SSE.2 crash-landed in the River Plym and

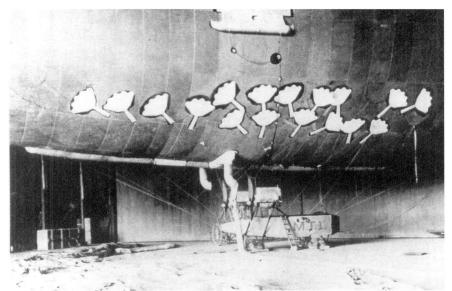

M.T.1 *seen at Mullion in early 1918 prior to its flight trials at the station. The engines and ballonet air scoops have been installed, while the network of* Eta *patches is clearly visible against the darker finish of the starboard side of the envelope. (Kind permission RNAS Culdrose)*

The first flight of M.T.1. This took place at Mullion on 4 March 1918. An interested group of handlers and observers are beneath the airship. Bombs are carried beneath the car. In the background can be distinguished the circular practice bombing area marked out on the south-western side of the station. (Kind permission RNAS Culdrose)

Mullion's own airship was redesignated SSE.2 shortly after the commencement of its flight trials, and is seen at the station during the spring of 1918. The envelope has received a new coat of dope that obscures the former clarity of the revised Eta patch layout, while the air scoops aft of the engines have been redesigned. Three main guy ropes are visible, each with its group of handlers. A fourth party attends the car of the airship while under the nose of the envelope stand several observers. (Royal Aeronautical Society)

Coastal Star Class Airship C*10 aloft during the summer of 1918, with Mullion's portable canvas Bessoneaux hangars in the background. The hangars were used to accommodate the aircraft based there. (J M Bruce/G S Leslie collection)

C*6 over the southern end of Mullion, her ballonet air scoop visible aft of the rear engine. Below, her naval handling crew, many wearing their white caps. The C* airships employed slimmer, more graceful envelopes than the earlier Coastals. (Helston Folk Museum)

C*6 surveys the seas from an altitude of some 400 ft, the Cornish coast forming the distant background. On the surface are several small vessels. (Ces Mowthorpe collection)

The mouth of the larger of Mullion's two airship sheds, summer 1918. To the left is C.9, while from within protrudes the nose of C*6. The huge doors of the shed are visible, as is the observation tower over the entrance. Just distinguishable below the envelope of C.9 are the white caps of her ground-handling crew. (Bruce Wood)

The car of SSZ.49 in the smaller of Mullion's sheds during the summer of 1918. Acoustic hydrophone sound detection equipment has recently been installed, and is visible here. The finned hydrophone was lowered into the water from the cable mounted on the reel behind the front seat of the car. Underwater sounds picked up by the hydrophone (including but not limited to those made by U-boats) were transmitted to the receiver manned by the crew member. (Author's collection)

was damaged while attempting to land during a storm. Rebuilt, the *Mullion Twin* completed a total of only 57 hours flying and during that time crashed once more; despite those two episodes her trials were held to be successful to the extent that she formed the basis for a new class of airship, the SST ('Twin').

It was intended to build 115 SSTs by mid-1919, in order to replace both Coastal and SSZ classes, but in the event only thirteen of the new type were produced because the war came to an end. Of these, SST.2 served at Toller, under the control of Mullion, also visiting the parent station and the outstation at Bochym Wood. Meanwhile, Flight Lieutenant Montagu went on to participate further in airship development before he died tragically in the disaster which befell the R.38 rigid airship over the River Humber on 23 August 1921.

Coastal Star (C*) Class airships also operated from Cornwall for a short time, during the closing stages of the war. The C* Class was something of a stop-gap between the Coastal Class and the North Sea Class; fielding of the latter was delayed by technical difficulties particularly with the drive-shaft arrangement. Only ten Coastal Star airships were built but the type was successful, its 210,000 cu ft envelope being longer and much more graceful in appearance than the earlier Coastal Class though still of trilobe arrangement, and containing six ballonets. The open car configuration was retained but the skinning was of plywood rather than the previous fabric, while triplex portholes were inserted into the car sides for an improved downward view and a triplex section was let into the floor to overcome the blind spot directly below the craft. Notably, provision was also made for the carriage of parachutes for the five crew, a rare concession at that time and a very welcome move away from earlier thinking.

Two C* airships were based in Cornwall, C*6 and C*10, during the summer and autumn of 1918. C*6 arrived at Mullion from Kingsnorth on 29 May 1918, where it remained until 20 August, then being obliged to return to Kingsnorth for repairs. Mid-October saw its return to Cornwall and it was finally deflated at Pulham airship station at the end of March 1919, having flown a total of 522 hours. C*10 served at Mullion as well as Bude, and latterly Toller, where it was eventually deleted from the strength of the RAF in October 1919.

A further device in the anti-submarine campaign was developed during the course of the war, in the form of no fewer than eleven various versions of the acoustic hydrophone. This equipment was very much to the forefront of the technology of the day, and was intended to allow surface vessels to detect the presence of U-boats by listening for noise emanating from their engines while submerged, though such a method was of course useless should the submarine not be under power. In an attempt to broaden the application of the new tool, airborne hydrophone trials took place with the code-name *Rubber Eel*, using Mullion's airships including C.23a and SSZ.49, and the results were considered sufficiently promising to plan the introduction of the new system to all SSZ ships. However, the Armistice brought these proposals to a prompt end.

RNAS Newlyn/Land's End during the first half of 1917. The station was situated on a small promontory on the western side of Mount's Bay, backing on to a quarry. Two Bessoneaux hangars were employed at first, later supplemented by a third, as seen here. Later a larger, more permanent hangar was also erected. The station featured a form of slipway employing rails running from the hangars to the water's edge; on this ran a launching trolley upon which sat the seaplane. Two aircraft are visible, one at the head of the slipway, the other between the hangars. (J M Bruce/G S Leslie collection)

The view east over Mount's Bay from the rear of the congested Newlyn hard standing, during the summer of 1917. The station's large shed was erected after the Bessoneaux hangars were found inadequate for the task of accommodating the aircraft. A tiny steam engine helps with the building work. Just visible in the background at the entrance to the Bessoneau hangar is a Short 184. In the distance, Mount's Bay.
(J M Bruce/G S Leslie collection)

PART TWO
THE AIRCRAFT DETERRENT

1 MULLION, AND NEW STATIONS

Though the local Cornish newspapers were virtually silent on activities at Mullion, the Government permitted the printing of (to say the least) sanitised information regarding the progress of the wider war. Among the aspects covered most prominently - though selectively - in papers parochial and national was the use of German Zeppelin rigid airships to carry out air-raids on Britain. This naturally was also one of the areas of greatest concern to the civilian home front, which indeed had experienced a powerful anticipatory fear of such attacks even before the outbreak of hostilities.

Pre-war, the growth of Imperial Germany's Zeppelin strength had been observed from overseas as one of the numerous frank indications of her expansionist aspirations. When the air-raids came, they generally concentrated on southern and eastern England though on 31 January 1916 nine Zeppelins struck at Liverpool, a display which demonstrated the capacity of the *genre* to travel

RNAS Tresco, with its main hangar under construction, during the summer of 1917. To the right of the hangar is the power station, the shadow from its chimney visible, while to the left is the hull of a Curtiss H.12 flying-boat. The slipway, running NNW - ESE, appears to have been completed; an H.12 is moored just to its left, using one tail and two wing-tip lines to the shore. A seemingly derelict hull sits on the beach at the bottom centre of the photograph, possibly H.12 8656. The personnel on the road to the right of the photograph are walking from the canteen area which is out of shot.
(J M Bruce/G S Leslie collection)

considerable distances in order to make such attacks provided the weather conditions were favourable. This new development in warfare was held up as a leading example of Teutonic frightfulness, fuelled and made more lurid by the British press than its consequence in terms of actual damage and fatalities might have warranted. The main effect of the raids was not the destruction or loss of life they inflicted but rather, their stunning emotional impact on a civilian population previously isolated from the consequences of wars invariably fought elsewhere, and the nation experienced feelings of outrage, helplessness and bewilderment.

In the light of the threat perceived by the authorities even as far west as Cornwall, and perhaps in an effort to be seen to be doing something to combat the putative danger there, by mid-May 1916 a powerful siren had been installed at Truro gasworks to alert people to any approaching Zeppelin. Later that month, what was quaintly described as an air-raid rehearsal had taken place in the city, though why the Germans should prefer to bomb Truro rather than, say, the shipping of Devonport or Falmouth, remained (necessarily) unclear.

During January 1917 the *Newquay Express* demonstrated one of the less considered reactions to the 'airship menace', when it advertised the opportunity to insure local properties against Zeppelin raids, available through Trethewey and Company, a newsagents situated at Mount Charles, near St Austell. The insurer was the *Daily News* and cover was also available against bombardment from the sea and shrapnel damage resulting from anti-aircraft fire. However, by the following June, the *Express* conceded the county should be a place safe from air-raids. The Zeppelins did not visit; bearing in mind the distance to Cornwall, with its sparse centres of population and its lack of industry, as well as the operational difficulties sometimes experienced by the Germans in mounting raids over even the much nearer south-east and eastern parts of Britain, the threat to the county was not real and no aerial defence force arrived for the purpose of shooting down airships.

It was not the possibility of air raids which brought aircraft to Cornwall, but the grave need to reinforce the U-boat searches carried out by the RNAS airships based there, as the anti-submarine campaign became ever more savage and its successful conclusion critical to the survival of Britain's war effort. On 1 February 1917, Germany declared a second phase of unrestricted submarine warfare, against all merchant vessels found in the waters surrounding Britain and Ireland. During the following month, enemy action accounted for 594,000 tons of merchant shipping of which 353,000 tons was British; in April a staggering 881,000 tons of shipping was lost of which 545,300 tons was British, the onslaught also naturally driving off scores of neutral ships from their intended British ports of destination. Thousands of seamen lost their lives during the period. The view expressed in some quarters (and indeed by the First Sea Lord Sir John Jellicoe, whose appointment immediately came under severe scrutiny) was that not only were such losses quite unsustainable but that if they continued the war would undoubtedly be lost, and sooner rather than later.

As one of the measures taken to help counter the appalling situation, on 29 March 1917 the First Sea Lord approved a proposal to populate Mullion, together with the stations at Prawle Point near Plymouth on the south Devonshire coast, and at Pembroke, with four aircraft each, in order to supplement the existing RNAS coastal patrol resources in those areas. This might in hindsight seem a very meagre

Right. A De Havilland DH.6 at Mullion; this example employs a four bladed propeller. Two young men stand nonchalantly in the foreground, one in part of a military uniform, the other in civvies, perhaps a local farmer's son. In the cockpit is a third person, who is wearing a naval peaked cap rather than a flying-helmet. (RCPS Research Project)

RNAS Tresco in mature state, seen from its northern side. The large metal hangar housing the twin-engined flying-boats has been completed. Immediately in front of the hangar are workshops. Behind the hangar, out of shot, is the power station and accommodation. The slipway is visible to the right. There appears to be very little activity – perhaps this photograph was taken early in the morning or even, possibly, following the end of hostilities. (R A Dorrien-Smith)

gesture but it was actually a reflection of the acute lack of resources elsewhere at that time - during their own horrendous campaign that April, the Royal Flying Corps alone lost no fewer than 316 aircraft, together with the vast majority of their crews.

In the spring of that year, therefore, Mullion's airship station commenced a second role, as an airfield, when four RNAS Sopwith 1½ Strutter single-engined biplanes arrived to assist with submarine patrols along the Cornish coast. Aircraft were sent partly because there was simply no time to build any further airships, and because in any case the design and performance of the Coastal Class was under some scrutiny by that point, while a choice of a possible replacement airship type was not fully resolved. The use of landplanes was a second choice, the Admiralty's natural preference being for seaplanes; however, it was conceded there were not sufficient of the latter available to divert to the area at that time.

During mid-April Mullion received two two-seat fighter versions of the 1½ Strutter (N5607 and N5608) and two single-seat bomber variants (N5601 and N5602). Two further examples, N5603 and N5604, both single-seat bombers, passed through Mullion in April, but were swiftly moved away to Prawle Point during the same month, where a similar force was being assembled. A fifth Mullion-based example, N5619, arrived at the end of April, while two more, N5623 and N5624, were erected at Mullion at the end of the month but were promptly posted to Prawle Point. When not on anti-U-boat patrols, the two-seat 1½ Strutters were occasionally employed on aerial photography and coastal mapping tasks.

RNAS Newlyn/Land's End. A very rare siting of a Fairey Hamble Baby seaplane, which carries the code '7'. It sits by the station's launching trolley, positioned between two Short 184s, both of which have their rangy wings folded. In the background is a third Short 184. (Peter Wearne)

RNAS Padstow/Crugmeer's primitive buildings (albeit an improvement on canvas) were employed to accommodate the more senior personnel. The windows appear to have no glass, but merely solid covers which can be raised or lowered. Duckboards have been set down to avoid the worst of the churned-up field. This photograph was taken in late 1918. (Malcolm McCarthy)

DH.6 C7847 *provides the backdrop to a small group plus pet photographed at Mullion during the summer of* 1918. *C7847 was powered by a Curtiss OX-2 engine and served with Nos 254 and 236 Squadrons. In the background are two further DH.6 examples and to the left a hangar.*
(J M Bruce/G S Leslie collection)

A single Bessoneau canvas hangar was erected in which to accommodate Mullion's Sopwiths, situated adjacent to the larger of the airship sheds. N5601 stayed for some time, eventually departing for Grain in February 1918 where it was used for flotation tests, but N5602 was written off in an accident on 2 May 1917. N5619 was moved to Prawle Point on 11 July 1917. During August, the RNAS pilots at Mullion were transferred to the Western Front as part of an attempt to bring the RNAS squadrons in France up to strength, and the aircraft at Mullion therefore lay idle before moving away. N5607 and N5608 both departed for the RNAS station at Eastchurch during mid-October of that year.

By November 1917 only two 1½ Strutters, N5619 and N5624 returned from Prawle Point, were based at Mullion, but de Havilland DH.6s, simple two-seat biplanes originally conceived for training purposes, began to arrive there early in the following year. Later, during May and June 1918, Nos 515 and 516 (Special Duties) Flights respectively were formed from the DH.6s. These aircraft were joined at Mullion by No 493 Flight, which employed de Havilland DH.9 two-seat biplanes, and which was formed in May. Subsequently all three Flights were joined together under No 254 Squadron Royal Air Force as part of the reorganisation of Britain's air services, but on 20 August this became No 236 Squadron, commanded by Major (later Wing Commander) R B B Colmore. Eventually, six Bessoneaux hangars were erected for the use of Mullion's aircraft, positioned between the north-western fence and the larger of the airship sheds. Additional accommodation for the pilots and ground crews was erected on the station, in the form of Armstrong huts and tents. Major Colmore went on to become the Officer Commanding at Mullion; post-war, tragically he died in the R.101 disaster.

RNAS Padstow/Crugmeer during the summer of 1918. The station employed three Bessoneaux hangars at first, but later a fourth was erected. To the left is a farm that abutted the station. The tents and some of the domestic buildings were placed rather hopefully in what there was of the lee of the hangars and the farm. Eleven DH.6s are visible at rest on the grass. (J M Bruce/G S Leslie collection)

The road junction leading to RNAS Padstow/Crugmeer, showing the tented accommodation for the other ranks, later in 1918. The nearby farm house is positioned on the left of the photograph while at the top, a Bessoneau hangar and two DH.6s are just visible. Additional buildings have been erected to the right of the photograph, which was taken from a DH. 6. (Malcolm McCarthy)

A *bombed-up* Short 184 *at rest at the end of the Newlyn slipway. Visible are the slipway rails and aircraft trolley cable assembly, as well as the tiny wheels of the trolley itself. In the background in Mount's Bay is a small naval vessel.* (Ian Stratford collection)

Mullion did not remain the sole centre of RNAS aircraft activity in Cornwall. As the need for a greater aerial presence there grew, the campaign against the U-boats was also fought from two further airfields established in Cornwall - at Newlyn and at Padstow - and from a station on Tresco, all these bases accommodating aircraft. A combined force was developed by the RNAS; floatplanes and landplanes employed on inshore patrols, airships, slow but with great endurance and large flying-boats which provided a swift long-range strike force and some of the heaviest aerial hitting power of the day.

RNAS Newlyn /Land's End was commissioned in January 1917, again a product of the Admiralty's urgent need to extend seaplane patrols further west in order to supplement the existing Channel defensive network. The base was situated two miles south of Penzance on the western side of Mount's Bay, despite its somewhat misleading title, and was built at great speed using much civilian labour. A narrow apron between Newlyn harbour and Carn Gwavas was utilised, a little to the south-east of the main pier there. Two (later three) Bessoneaux hangars were erected for the incoming aircraft and officers' quarters established in nearby York House; the men were billeted mostly in Penzance. A slipway was hurriedly constructed facing to the north-east, which consisted of two rails supported by sleepers and mounting a wooden wheeled platform designed to bear the aircraft. At the top of the slipway was laid an area of hard-standing. Later, a second slipway was constructed to the north of the first. Short 184 two seat biplane floatplanes started to arrive, the first, 8049 and 8350, on 20 January. At the onset of the station's life its aircraft were surrounded by a shambles of uncompleted construction work.

With the arrival of further aircraft the hangars at Newlyn became so cramped that from time to time some of the Shorts were stored in the Trinity House buildings at Penzance. A 180 ft x 60 ft shed was subsequently built at the station to house six seaplanes. The occasional Curtiss H.12 flying-boat from Tresco also visited; 8654 arrived in fog in May of that year, while a further example visited after running out of fuel during June 1918. In the meantime, from the end of May 1918 the resident Newlyn Shorts had been assembled as Nos 424 and 425 Flights, each intended to operate six aircraft, though their real strengths were always lower. On 20 August No 235 Squadron RAF was formed using these Flights, under the command of Major A K Robertson. One, possibly two, Short 320 floatplanes, of similar configuration to the Short 184, are thought to have made brief visits at that time.

At least two Parnall-built Fairey Hamble Baby single-engined biplane floatplanes (N1191 and N1205) also operated from Newlyn. N1191 arrived during July 1917 but was temporarily attached to Tresco, completing its service in Cornwall during December, while N1205 arrived in November 1917 for a brief stay until the following February. A third Hamble Baby, the Fairey-built N1322, crashed *en route* for service at Newlyn in July 1917 and in the event did not operate there.

Shortly after the formation of the South Western Group, during the spring of 1917, a process began of drawing up a more formal system of patrols than hitherto for the aerial forces gathered at Mullion and Newlyn - and later, those at Tresco and Padstow. The patrol patterns were designed by Major Colmore at Mullion, and consisted of three classes - 'Routine', 'Emergency' and 'Contact', the last-named being applicable to seaplanes only. The arrangement of Routine patrols allowed for three standard patrols from each station in the Group, such that provided each station sent at least one aircraft or airship on a particular patrol, practically the maximum patrol area would be covered. Patrols were carried out morning and evening - sometimes commencing very early in the morning - as far as the weather and the condition of the machines allowed.

Commanding Officers at the stations were instructed to keep, where possible, one seaplane or landplane in readiness for Emergency patrols, which could be ordered by the Group headquarters on receipt of intelligence reports. Such Emergency patrols might also be undertaken following receipt of reliable local information. Aeroplane Contact patrols took place in co-operation with the Captain (D) 4th Destroyer Flotilla, based at Penzance, using one or more destroyers. If more than one destroyer were employed, these craft would sail in parallel at a distance apart of typically eight miles, for around 45 miles from port, the aircraft patrolling in a zigzag pattern over the seas between them, and maintaining contact with the surface vessels at fixed points (either three, six or nine

A Curtiss H.12 *moored off RNAS Tresco, summer 1917. Two underwing bombs are visible. The port engine is under power but those on board are not in flying dress.* (J M Bruce/G S Leslie collection)

No 234 Squadron F.3 N4415 mounted on its beaching trolley, and parked on RNAS Tresco's hard standing, summer 1918. Just ahead of the aircraft is the station's slipway, while behind it is a second beaching trolley. In the background, some of the Tresco workshops. The main hangar is just behind the camera. (Chris Ashworth)

miles) along the route. The system of patrols was altered and amplified during the first half of 1917, and finally standardised by a set of printed orders which were approved by Devonport in August.

While the seaplanes at Newlyn were developing their tactics, a 20-acre flying-boat site had been formed at Tresco. As early as 1916 a small number of Short 184 floatplanes had been posted to the Isles of Scilly but had received considerable punishment while moored in the exposed St Mary's Roads, an area which provided little protection from the changeable and sometimes fierce weather conditions experienced in that part of the world, and after a brief stay the aircraft were removed. However, the increasingly severe Allied shipping losses during the following year prompted the Admiralty to try again and that time it was concluded flying-boats should be sent.

During January 1917 an RNAS advance party was despatched to Porth Mellon, situated on the western side of St Mary's. The first aircraft to be posted to the second base were Curtiss H.12s, 8654 and 8664, large twin-engined maritime patrol flying-boats. They arrived on 18 February, being followed by 8652 on 25 February and 8656 on 28 February, the latter carrying the commanding officer of the new station, Squadron Commander Hope-Vere; later that day 8652 flew the first operational patrol. However, that site was very quickly also found too challenging from an environmental point of view, and following the suggestion of Flight Commander R B Maycock, a more sheltered area was found on the western side of Tresco, delineated by Hacket Town Lane, Great Pool, Pool Road, New Grimsby and the coastline, and facing Bryher. It was decided to establish yet another temporary base and see whether that would be any more successful than its predecessors.

Happily, the third site survived the rigors of the weather and was deemed a success. RNAS Tresco was in theory operational by the end of February 1917, though at that time it suffered from scant facilities indeed. These consisted of one Bessoneau hangar, some tents, and a few wooden buildings. During those early days, the station's personnel were ferried over daily from their St Mary's billets. Six H.12s were nominally on the station's strength.

While Tresco was still very much in its infancy, during March 1917 two destroyers arrived at Scilly to conduct experiments with kite balloons. It was intended the kite balloons be towed from the destroyers while underway, and used to spot for submarines. The ships stayed for four weeks before leaving for Plymouth where further tests were carried out.

In the spring of 1917 it was decided to put Tresco on a more permanent footing, and buildings of greater substance, a canteen, and two metal framed hangars, were erected by No 1 Air Construction Section RNAS over the following summer. In addition, a substantial slipway was built to allow the launching and retrieval of the large flying-boats of the day, together with a small floating dock arrangement intended to facilitate servicing activities. An area to the south-east of the station was cleared to enable calls from passing airships.

By August 1917 a further refined method of allocating patrol patterns had been established by the South Western Group. These were known as Series I (or Inner) Patrols and Series II (or Outer) Patrols, large mostly rectangular areas covering the perceived regions of most danger from the underwater marauders, extending some 80 miles south-west of the Scilly Isles, south from the Lizard, south-east toward Exmouth, across the Bristol Channel and north-east to Barnstaple. Each of the three Inner and three Outer Patrol areas were divided into either two or three sub-areas

RNAS Tresco viewed from the southern side. The accommodation is visible, and has expanded significantly compared with the air-shot of the station, taken earlier in its career. Beyond is the power house with its chimney outlined against the large hangar seen side-on. To the left is the slipway and the area of water used by the aircraft. (R A Dorrien-Smith)

referred to as A, B and where appropriate C, while the airship patrol routes within each were numbered 1,2 or 3, so that a patrol could be linked to a particular area by, for example, the reference Series I (Inner) Patrol 2A, or Series II (Outer) Patrol 1B (see Appendix 7). In addition to this scheme, by the early part of 1918, a mapped system of large squared areas over the seas around the Cornish coast had been drawn up for use by the U-boat hunters. Employing these, it was possible to carry out reasonably precise patrols in areas not covered by the Series Patrol system, and the two arrangements continued in use side-by-side as the tactics of the RNAS continued to develop.

Over the summer of 1918, F.3 flying-boats started to arrive for service at Tresco. The F.3 was a twin-engined aircraft of somewhat similar aspect to the H.12 though a much better all-round performer. The first example, N4000, was delivered to Tresco on 29 July via Cattewater in Devon. Though it was intended that twelve F.3s serve at Tresco, that strength was never achieved. Nonetheless, from May 1918, four Flights, Nos 350 - 353, were formed, on 31 May, 30 June, 15 September and 30 September respectively. Over that period the aircraft types serving at Tresco embraced the Short 184, as well the H.12s and eight F.3s including for a time N4234 sporting a turquoise and white dazzle colour scheme, akin to those of the RNAS Felixstowe-based F-boats. No 234 Squadron formed on 20 August using these Flights, under the command of R B Maycock, who by that time held the rank of Major. The two Flights existing at the time of the Squadron's formation retained their identities within its framework; indeed, Nos 352 and 353 Flights, formed after the Squadron itself, ceased to exist only when it disbanded in mid-May 1919. The diminutive FBA single-engined flying-boat is also said to have served in small numbers.

*

During January 1918, of the shipping losses inflicted by U-boats around the British Isles some 60% were suffered within ten miles of the shore. The submarines, frustrated by the introduction of the convoy system which left wide expanses of seas free of shipping, moved their operational territory much closer to the British shoreline and its ports than hitherto. A new, very urgent need therefore emerged for the RNAS to provide regular inshore aerial coastal patrols around the British Isles. In order to carry out such patrols off the Cornish coast, a 50-acre airfield was established near Padstow, employing three (later four) Bessoneaux hangars, while wooden buildings and tents were erected to accommodate officers and men respectively. Later a few brick-built huts appeared, their roofs formed from curved corrugated iron. A landing run of some 1,500 ft across the cliff top was made available, very exposed and on sloping ground, which of course was far from ideal. The new base was also close to the hamlet of Crugmeer and was commissioned in March 1918 as RNAS Padstow/Crugmeer. Originally the name Trevose Head had been considered, but Trevose Head is some five miles from the station site and that suggestion was abandoned. DH.6 two-seat biplanes began to arrive shortly after the new base opened and at its peak the station accommodated around 180 personnel.

On 31 May Nos 500 and 501 Flights went operational at Padstow, on DH.6s - usually, around a dozen aircraft were stationed there at a time. As well as the DH.6s, occasional visitors arrived in the form of the odd Avro 504K, Sopwith Pup and (allegedly) Curtiss JN-4 aircraft, as well as SSZ Class airships. On 2 May a DH.9 flight formed at Padstow and this became No 494 Flight in mid June.

Left. *Tresco's H.12 N4341 was also known as* The Fililu. *This example completed a total flying time of 239.22 hours between March and October 1918, making 85 patrols from the Scilly Islands during that period. It is seen here moored adjacent to Tresco's slipway, with its beaching crew in attendance.* (R. Dorrien-Smith)

From 20 August the Flights fell under No 250 Squadron RAF. Initially the squadron was commanded by Major R E Orton, but later by Major F Warren Merriam AFC, who pre-war had made a name in Falmouth as a motorist before travelling to Brooklands to learn to fly. Prior to assuming his command at Padstow, as a Flight Lieutenant Warren Merriam had flown 1½ Strutters from Mullion.

On 1 April 1918, the Royal Air Force came into being and on the same day, the administrative control of both the former Royal Naval Air Service and the Royal Flying Corps across the whole of the south west of England was placed in the hands of the newly-created No 9 (Operations) Group, based at Mount Wise, Devonport. This was evidently a clumsy arrangement and in August 1918 the resources were split. No 71 (Operations) Wing was created, its headquarters at Penzance, one of ten such Wings and reporting to 9 Group, which also assumed control of the new No 72 (Operations) Wing, the latter having its command centre at RNAS Cattewater, a mile or so south of Plymouth at Mount Batten. Of course, it was not possible to implement these paper changes in organisation immediately. In any case, within Cornwall the operational activities of aircraft and airships remained unaltered and continued under the administration of the Naval authorities at Plymouth.

2 OPERATIONS AND ACCIDENTS

Cornwall's DH.6s were unfortunately almost as much a burden as a fighting force. The DH.6 was a languid performer and its niggardly powerplant frequently of poor reliability, while many examples also suffered from advanced structural problems. The aircraft was soon given the sobriquet *Clutching Hand*, a comment on the appearance of its acute wing camber but also perhaps suggestive of a spectre snatching its prey - in the form of the crew. Carrying any offensive stores was a great undertaking, but a maximum bombload of around 100 lb was just about manageable provided the pilot flew alone. Occasionally, examples were used merely as unarmed signalling aircraft, an observer operating an Aldis lamp in order to communicate with those below.

Patrols were typically of two hours' duration, covering an inshore area some fifteen to twenty miles wide, and naturally were carried out at low-level to maximise the chance of observing the enemy - in any case, the DH.6's ability to climb while carrying the necessary bombload was feeble. At Padstow, it was soon found that should aircraft return having retained their bombs, often they were unable to gain sufficient height to clear the cliffs on which the station was situated, necessitating a turbulent final stage to the airfield along the conveniently-situated valley just south of Gunver Head. A number of the personnel posted to the RNAS's home coastal stations had previously suffered injuries which deemed them unfit for front-line service, but in fact the constant patrols in such difficult circumstances would have taxed many in good health.

Accidents involving the Padstow-based DH.6s were numerous. One example, C6678, ran out of fuel while patrolling on 20 May 1918 and landed in the sea; a passing vessel towed the aircraft back to land seemingly undamaged where it was dried out and re-entered service - nine days following that episode it was reported missing and was never seen again. On 28 May, C6683 made a forced landing in the sea. Another crashed at Trethewell, just north of St Eval on the north coast - local man Jim Leverton, posted to guard the completely inert aircraft, advised the small crowd which duly

Right. Short 184 N2988 *at Newlyn, parked between the Bessoneaux hangars at the southern side of the station. It is fitted with wireless, and rests on a simple beaching chassis. Behind the hangar, the house on the incline became the officers' mess. N2988 served at Newlyn with 235 Squadron between October 1918 and January 1919. (Reg Watkiss)*

Damaged Tresco-based Felixstowe F.3, photographed at Mount's Bay, summer 1918. The aircraft has been moored just off the shore, but sadly, its hull has been damaged and has ingested a considerable amount of water. The lower wings and tailplane have disappeared beneath the surface. (Reg Watkiss)

assembled to "stand back from the 'ropeller". C5194 experienced a forced landing, again in the sea on 4 July but was salved by the collier *Brook* and taken to Newlyn, its pilot free of injury and his spirits at least undampened. Two days later C6682 crashed three miles south of Bude and was destroyed - but again, the pilot was unhurt. On 23 July C5205 struck C7858 while landing at Padstow, tumbled into the sea and was totally wrecked, though its very fortunate crew of two somehow survived their ordeal. On 21 September a serviceman was killed in a propeller accident at the station.

Mullion's DH.6 complement was no better off. On 8 July 1918, C7799 crashed into the Lizard cliffs, perhaps as a result of being unable to make the necessary altitude to clear them on its return to Mullion; the pilot was never recovered. On 30 June C7844 sank after alighting on the sea, also following engine failure, while on 14 August C7842 of No 236 Squadron also experienced an immersion, yet again due to engine failure, but stayed afloat and was salved by a passing French trawler. During September 1918, both C6588 and C6661 experienced such failure over the sea, and were towed ignominiously into Mullion harbour. The quite appalling unreliability of the American Curtiss OX-2 and OX-5 engines which powered all of the above examples, bar C6588 (80 hp Renault), was surely demonstrated no less graphically than during the operations of the DH.6 from Cornwall's long coastline, and the courage of its pilots can only be wondered at. Finally, on Armistice Day, C7645 crashed and was slightly damaged - following an engine failure.

Offensive actions (at the enemy) by the DH.6s were very few but C5206 from No 250 Squadron piloted by Captain H Goodfellow released a bomb at a U-boat sighted three miles off Trevose Head on 23 July 1918, while C7849, also of No 250 Squadron and flown by Lieutenant A C Tremellon dropped a 65 lb bomb on a U-boat while on patrol on 27 July, though neither attempt produced a clear result. Lieutenant H H Shorter flying C5207, from Padstow too, was fortunate enough to observe a U-boat off Newquay on 13 August, and pressed home the attack, dropping two small bombs - but infuriatingly, both failed to explode. Ten days later, as if exhausted by its effort, C5207 too force-landed in the sea.

The value of the DH.6 patrols was not in their actual offensive power, which was on the slim side of negligible, but in the psychological threat of the possibility they might be in the vicinity, which helped dissuade the U-boats from surfacing, or pressing home their attacks as remorselessly as they would had air cover not been provided - even such cover as the DH.6s were able to manage. A total of some 69 DH.6s served at Padstow and Mullion.

The DH.9 was a far more competent aircraft than the DH.6, of much better construction and reliability though it did suffer from idiosyncratic properties of its own, particularly concerning its powerplant. A handful of attacks were made by the DH.9s on suspected U-boats. On 28 July 1918 D2964 of No 250 Squadron attacked a submarine sighted at 5028N 0515W though again, without clear signs of success. Altogether, 30 DH.9s served at the RNAS's Cornish stations. One example, D1714 of No 250 Squadron, crashed on landing at Padstow on 16 June 1918 and its two crewmen were injured. On 24 July, D2963, also operated by No 250 Squadron, force-landed in the sea and one

DH.6 coded '23', probably Mullion-based 236 Squadron's C7645, photographed after a nose-over during the autumn of 1918. The rudder has been recovered and placed in the foreground. (Author's collection)

of its bombs exploded on hitting the water; surprisingly, the two men aboard survived. D1712 of No 236 Squadron crashed in Poldhu Creek, just north of Mullion village, on 15 October, again fortunately without loss of life.

At Newlyn, the Short 184s saw a number of actions. On 16 March 1917 8350 bombed a U-boat 10 miles south-south-east of Dodman Point, though without achieving a positive result on that occasion. Three days later, the crew of N1614 were rescued by the Falmouth trawler *Gowan* after their aircraft had suffered engine failure and crashed in the sea. On 29 March 8049 had to be towed into Falmouth following an engine failure, and was damaged during a freak snowstorm there on 1 April. N1605 and N1604 attacked submarines on 16 August and 8 September respectively, both off the Wolf Rock, but neither attempt was conclusive. On 7 September N1636 suffered engine failure resulting in a forced landing at sea, but the aircraft was towed into Newlyn by the ML350.

On 19 December, however, a more successful strike was made when N1606 severely damaged a U-boat ten miles south-west of the Lizard. The submarine had been following a convoy of merchantmen and the aircraft observed the track of its torpedo, which fortunately missed its target. Following the seaplane's attack, air bubbles and oil were observed rising to the surface of the water. However, the same aircraft was less fortunate when making a subsequent attack on 2 January 1918 - both its 100 lb bombs failed to explode. The following day, Short 184 N1603 from RNAS Cattewater crashed in open seas and sank after its engine caught fire, but its two fortunate crewmen were rescued by the Greek vessel SS *Kanaris* and were landed at Falmouth.

Left. *A Curtiss OX-powered DH.6, employing a two-bladed propeller, serves as a photographic backdrop at Padstow during the summer of 1918. Behind are two further aircraft. The farmhouse adjacent to the station is visible on the left. (Malcolm McCarthy)*

Below. *A Short 184 at rest on the trolley at the top of the slipway at Newlyn, mounting a bomb and a depth charge. In the foreground are three 112 lb HE RL (High Explosive, Royal Laboratories) Mark 3 bombs. (J M Bruce/G S Leslie collection)*

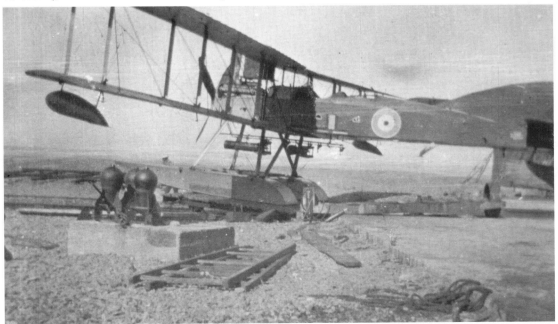

An incident developed on 3 March 1918 involving Newlyn's Short 184 N1606, flown that day by American Ensign Benjamin Lee accompanied by RNAS observer Sub-Lieutenant Rowley, when the pair became lost while patrolling the Land's End area in deteriorating weather and light. They reached the treacherous waters off the Eddystone lighthouse and landed but struck an outcrop while attempting to find shelter on the water, and severely damaged both floats. The lighthouse keepers, meanwhile, had witnessed events and were able to get a life-buoy to Lee, though Rowley was lost, and later received a letter of commendation from the Secretary of the US Navy.

Meanwhile, the Shorts were involved in further actions. N1618 released a 100 lb and a 65 lb bomb at a U-boat on 24 March 1918, N1609 dropped two 100 lb bombs at a sighting on 29 April, N1767 attacked a submarine on 6 May, though one bomb released failed to explode. N1616 claimed a suspected sinking on 16 May, using two 100 lb bombs against a U-boat spied off the north Cornish coast and subsequently sighting an oil slick, while N2631 and N2958 made two separate attacks on 30 June. N1770 attacked a slick on 13 July, being unsure as to its origin but not wishing to lose a possible opportunity, though there were no indications following that strike that a U-boat had been present.

Aircraft from Tresco also engaged the submarines on a number of occasions, again with mixed results. During 24 May 1917, H.12 8654 attacked a submarine which, possibly damaged by some previous incident, chose not to dive but instead fought back against the aircraft, using its deck armament. Not only did the two 100 lb bombs aimed from the aircraft miss their target, but the Germans' decision to slog it out somewhat surprisingly proved the right one; their fire hit the flying-boat's starboard engine

Short 184 N1604 coded '9', seen perched on its launching trolley at the head of Newlyn's slipway with crew on board, summer 1917. It is under power, and bombs are mounted between its floats.
(J M Bruce/G S Leslie collection)

A DH.9 *of No 494 Flight at Padstow, summer* 1918. *The aircraft is armed with underwing bombs. Behind, a DH.6, property of either* 500 *or* 501 *Flight, also based at Padstow.* (Malcolm McCarthy)

radiator and the engineer was obliged to climb onto the wing to fit a make-shift bung. The aircraft made one more bombing run but with equal lack of success, before the crew decided to return to base in view of the damage sustained to their aircraft. Following that disappointment, however, on 27 May H.12 8656 spotted a surfaced U-boat and quickly dropped two 100 lb bombs, both of which struck forward of the conning-tower; the submarine sank rapidly after its stern came high out of the water, and the flying-boat crew all received medals. Two days later 8656 made a suspected sighting and again, bombs were released. Despite the emergence of an oily patch it was felt a claim only for a possible sinking could be made.

On 25 June, 8665 released three 100 lb bombs on a U-boat which was about to attack a hospital ship 10 miles north of Cape Cornwall, and though there was no evidence of destruction, the attack succeeded in driving it off. H.12 8680 dropped three 100 lb bombs at a U-boat sighted 55 miles south-south-west of the Scilly Islands on 21 August and on 14 October dropped four such bombs on a submarine spied 15 miles south-west of St Mary's. During a patrol on 18 October, 8656 released four 100 lb bombs on a submarine 35 miles south-west of Bishop Rock and 8686 attacked a U-boat 30 miles south-west of St Mary's, perhaps the same vessel; following the latter attack, oil and air bubbles were observed rising from the damaged U-boat.

On 10 May 1918 Tresco-based H.12B N4341 attacked the U-103 using two 230 lb bombs, which damaged it before HMS *Olympic* arrived to finish it off. 23 July witnessed a take-off in very rough seas by N4341, made so as to provide an escort for an incoming convoy. The escort flight lasted four hours until finally the convoy approached the safety of the coast. During the flight, the aircraft managed to

Padstow hosts a rare visitor in the form of a Sopwith Pup. Two naval personnel pose for their photograph, one recovering from an injury to his arm. In the background is a resident DH.6 and beyond, a Bessoneau hangar. (Author's collection)

DH.6 C5194 on Newlyn's hard standing, following a forced landing at sea on 4 July 1918. The aircraft was taken in tow by the collier Brook and brought back to safety. It is surprisingly intact, the visible damage being limited to loss of some fuselage decking by the cockpit and near the tailplane. Behind are resident Short 184s. (J M Bruce/G S Leslie collection)

destroy several mines with machine-gun fire as well as keeping a look-out for U-boats. This mission earned signalled congratulations from 9 Group Headquarters.

On 30 August an inconclusive attack was made by F.3 N4238 on a U-boat sighted in mid ocean between the tip of Cornwall and Pembroke, while on 7 September the same aircraft spotted the White Star liner *Persic* crippled and under attack by a submarine, just west of the Isles of Scilly. The U-boat was forced to retreat under the force of bombs dropped (and subsequently sank), while wireless messages made by the aircraft alerted vessels to the need to organise a tow to St Mary's for the *Persic*. One of the final attacks of the war was made by H.12B N4341 on 11 October, when it detected the wake of a submarine some four miles ahead of Convoy HH.71. Subsequently, oil was spotted on the surface of the water and the signs were that the U-boat had slunk away.

As was to be expected of any station on a war footing, especially one operating under such difficult and isolated conditions, there were several accidents among the Tresco-based aircraft, some of them serious. On 11 March 1917 H.12 8652 had hurriedly to be beached at Newlyn after it started to sink in Mount's Bay, while on 9 May, H.12 8664 crashed and exploded during a gale, one mile south-west off Gugh Island, Scilly, its three crew that day being killed. In foggy conditions on 5 June, H.12 8654 landed off Trevose Head near Padstow on the north Cornish coast. It proved impossible to make a return home by air, but remarkably, the machine was successfully towed the considerable distance back to Tresco, though its wings and tail were damaged in the process. On 16 December gales lashed the station and three moored-out H.12s (8665, 8680 and 8686) were destroyed in the 100 mph winds, parting their mooring cables, turning turtle and being thrown onto the beach inverted - the same gale slightly damaged H.12 8674. During January and February of the following year, the weather remained so poor around the Scilly Isles that only one patrol from Tresco was recorded over the period.

H.12 8675 was destroyed on 14 June 1918, when it caught fire following a forced landing attributed

The officers and men of No 234 Squadron congregate for a photographic session at Tresco's large hangar during 1918. (Via Chris Ashworth)

to a crankshaft failure just off the Islands, and two crewmen were drowned, including the W/T rating. The following month, on 6 July, Newlyn's Short 184 N2963 failed to return and during the resultant search for survivors, one of the aircraft despatched, Tresco's F.3 N4234, suffered a petrol leak and was forced to alight in heavy seas. Though it subsequently sank under tow, its crew were rescued by the *Braemar Castle*, a hospital ship. On 7 August, a mere ten days after its arrival at Tresco, F.3 N4000 developed the phenomenon known as 'porpoising' while taking-off, and bounced itself across the water until its hull gave way; it had swiftly to be beached on Samson. Fortunately on that occasion there appear to have been no fatalities.

On 22 August N4001 was lost when it crashed just off the station following a failure of the starboard engine, and sank while on tow though again, the crew survived. On 23 October F.3 N3238 ran out of fuel and put down at sea but that time a successful tow was made back to Tresco. Certainly the long periods spent moored out in New Grimsby's harbour did not help operations, for the soakage of water into the wooden hulls of the flying-boats, coupled with corrosion of metal parts, was considerable. The last wartime patrol from Tresco, escorting a merchant convoy, was made on 10 November. Over the period of operations from Tresco, very much the most active of its aircraft was H.12 N4341, which arrived at the station during March 1918 and by the following October had put in almost 240 flying hours on patrol.

Right. *Short 184 N1608 coded '4', parked on its chassis at the entrance to one of Newlyn's hangars. Gazing at its bomb-load, a member of the ground staff lounges unconcernedly over a float. (Reg Watkiss)*

Short 184 N1254 at the water's edge, Newlyn, 1918. The aircraft wears the code '2' and is armed with two bombs. The pilot poses with a colleague and a dog. In the background can be seen the Newlyn harbour wall. (Peter Wearne)

Other aeronautical activities in Cornwall during the First World War included the work carried out by No 16 Balloon Base, stationed at Merifield (now known as Maryfield), near Torpoint on the western banks of the Tamar. Though it was situated on Cornish soil, the Balloon Base was not part of No 71 (Operations) Wing but came under No 72 Wing at RNAS Cattewater, just across the Sound. The base also ran a sub-station at Torquay. The Merifield site consisted of two areas totalling 13 acres, equipped with six balloon sheds, stores and crew rooms. Personnel were accommodated aboard the hulk HMS *Valiant*. The unit deployed six kite balloons (one permanently detached to Berry Head), intended to provide warnings of impending attacks on the local shipping.

Early during the final year of the war, two RNAS aircraft storage depots were established at the south-eastern end of the county, one at Tregantle Fort, situated by the St Germans River some three miles west of Torpoint, the other at Withnoe, just south of Freathy in Whitsand Bay. These depots generally supported the seaplane station at Cattewater, but were also used to house several ex-RFC DH.6s, B2944, B2945, B2946, B2947, B2948 and B2949: these aircraft arriving in March.

Sporadic aeronautical movements were carried out on the River Fal, where small numbers of seaplanes (probably Short 184s) were sometimes observed moored between Flushing and Falmouth; that location was occasionally used as a stopping-off point for deliveries proceeding further west (for example, by Short 184 N2919 *en route* for Newlyn), and as a bolt-hole when sudden changes of weather were encountered while on patrol. Short 184 N1601 visited Looe during March 1918, while Newquay also hosted a single-engined floatplane during the spring of 1918, almost certainly another Short 184.

Padstow, summer 1918. A cheerful pilot prepares to carry out a patrol in his DH. 6. He is well wrapped against the elements, with leather flying helmet and coat. (Malcolm McCarthy)

PART THREE
AFTERMATH

I THE WAR ENDS

On 7 November 1918, in a fund-raising event typical of the continuing home front war effort, the Bude Airship Station Concert Party provided entertainment at Stratton's Lecture Hall, and contributions were made to the Flying Services Fund. Just four days later, at eleven o'clock on Monday 11 November, the Armistice came into effect. As elsewhere, in Cornwall there were immediate scenes of jubilation and thanksgiving as hatless, flag-waving crowds gathered in Truro, where the business premises shut for the day, while spontaneous demonstrations of joy broke out too in the towns and villages across the county. Church services, fireworks displays and carnivals were organised. In the continuing pursuit of raising funds for needy causes, however, 21 November witnessed a concert at Launceston Town Hall, again given by the Bude Concert Party, that time in aid of incapacitated ex-servicemen; no doubt the participants and audience raised the roof with celebrations that night.

Naturally, both airship and aircraft patrols diminished sharply once it had been established that the U-boat commanders at sea had been apprised of the situation. During the first ten months of 1918, Mullion had returned 7,936 flying hours, more than any other RNAS airship station over that period. By the time of the Armistice, many of Mullion's airships were worn out or had been transferred away. Of the Coastals, only C.2 was flying there, together with seven SSZs, plus C*6, SSE.2 and SST.2 generally based at Toller. Those airships which had survived the course of the war were disposed of

Summer 1922: during the trip to the Isles of Scilly, the RAF Seaplane Development Flight's Short Cromarty N120 was holed on a reef and immersed up to its lower wings. Though the Cromarty was subsequently beached at St Mary's, as seen here, it was later scrapped as beyond economic repair. In the meantime, it provided an object of literally enormous interest for the local children.
(J M Bruce/G H Leslie collection)

during the following months. SSZ.75 made a forced landing at Padstow during December having only arrived for service at Mullion on 9 November - it flew a mere 43 hours that year. Fittingly, SSE.2 performed the station's last airship flight, on 25 January 1919. By then, Mullion men had been awarded no fewer than four DSCs, three DSMs and nine other 'mentions'.

During 1919, aviation retreated from Cornwall as swiftly as it had arrived, though isolated aircraft deliveries continued in the face of the general withdrawal; DH.9 H4284 was posted to Mullion during December 1918, and subsequently moved to Padstow. The creation of Mullion's airship station had been a wartime expedient and it quickly ran down after the Armistice. Only desultory flying was carried out and this sometimes took the form of attempts to spot and destroy mines left over from hostilities. On 18 January 1919 DH.9 C1304 spun in on take-off with one fatality - and No 236 Squadron disbanded in mid May. The base was gradually dismantled over the summer of 1919 and fell into disrepair, its work all but forgotten. The Bessoneaux hangars and tents were the first to be removed from the site, followed by the gas-producing equipment and the more significant wooden buildings. Some of the remaining buildings were subsequently stripped of useful parts by entrepreneurial locals. The main airship shed was eventually moved to Padstow, where it formed the basis of the bus station there. A short distance away from Mullion, the meagre facilities at Bochym began gently to revert to woodland.

On the north east Cornish coast, the influenza epidemic which had broken out across various parts of the country during September 1918 made its presence felt at the Bude outstation, where sadly, numbers of men succumbed. The site had never received any buildings stouter than wooden huts, and once the aviators had left, rapidly began to fade away. The huts were taken into use for agricultural purposes, and survived in that capacity for some years. The outstations at Toller and Upton were also abandoned shortly after hostilities ceased.

Newlyn too began to wind down. On 17 December, Short 184 N2979 of No 235 Squadron suffered engine failure and was towed back to the station, though it sank during the journey; resuscitated, the aircraft was able to soldier on, but following the Armistice the patrols were far less frequent and there was no longer any obligation to take to the air in poor weather. Newlyn was decommissioned during February 1919 and its Bessoneaux hangars removed, while No 235 Squadron disbanded on 22 February.

Padstow remained open until March 1919 but very little flying was carried out and No 250 Squadron also disbanded during mid May. The station's airship mooring mast was liberated, purchased for scrap by Mr Richard Parkyn Snr, landlord of the nearby Farmer's Arms public house at St Merryn cross roads, where it was left discarded in front of outbuildings on the road verge for many years. Tresco's No 234 Squadron also disbanded during mid-May as that station closed. The balloon site at Merifield was abandoned. No 9 (Operations) Group, together with No 71 (Operations) Wing was dissolved during the summer.

However, that was not quite the end of the story. Following its withdrawal from the Duchy, the RAF briefly returned to Newlyn and St Mary's during August and September 1922, in the form of the Seaplane Development Flight, commanded by Sqn Ldr R B Maycock OBE, who previously had helped establish RNAS Tresco during 1917. The Flight consisted of four large flying-boats; Felixstowe F.5 N4038, Felixstowe F.5 N4839 powered by Napier Lion engines, Phoenix P.5 Cork III N87 and Short Cromarty N120. Setting out from Calshot, the aircraft were followed by several support vessels - HMS *Ark Royal*, the parent ship, the destroyer HMS *Tintagel* and a floating dock towed by the tug

HMS *St Martin*. The purpose of their visit was to gain experience in the operation of flying-boats while isolated from their usual stations, instead employing ships to provide base facilities. Eighteen days were spent at the Isles of Scilly, the Flight arriving on 21 August and anchoring in St Mary's Roads, despite the unfavourable experiences of the RNAS in mooring their Short 184s there during 1916, and indeed this unsheltered area proved a severe test of the seaworthiness of the aircraft.

The visit to St Mary's was interrupted by a brief trip to Mount's Bay. Though the old Newlyn/Land's End station had been abandoned since 1919, the site had remained on the Air Ministry's emergency base list. All four aircraft visited, but the assessment of Newlyn concluded it was no longer suitable for operations, being situated adjacent to busy harbour areas, and having negligible space on its narrow apron for aircraft any larger than the Shorts which had originally populated the base. At St Mary's, because of the wind it was not always possible to use the floating dock for maintenance and repair work; such activities had frequently to be undertaken on the beach or in a more sheltered natural pool nearby.

Unfortunately, a storm blew up during the time the aircraft were moored out and though all four survived, the Cromarty was subsequently taxied onto a reef and severely damaged the underside of its hull, sinking up to its lower wing in the water. It had quickly to be beached at St Mary's, where an inspection revealed the damage was beyond economic repair, and was broken up *in situ*, its remains being salved by the *Ark Royal*. Despite that episode, however, the visit was considered useful and though the number of hours flown were few, valuable experience was gained in handling the 'boats in such a remote location.

Some eighteen years later, during the Second World War, a Chain Home radar station was established over the summer of 1940 at Drytree on Goonhilly Downs, the highest spot on the Lizard, following the fall of France. The Drytree personnel, which included several WAAFs, used a few of the buildings then surviving on the nearby site of the old RNAS Mullion.

Also at that time, an experimental balloon station was established on part of the defunct Mullion base. The balloons were used for tests associated with the calibration of the radar equipment situated at Drytree. The station employed temporary huts, and some further buildings remaining from the First World War occupation. Experiments using kites also took place at Mullion. The hopeful intention was to employ the kites in lifting cables mounting small bombs, and so form a protective aerial barrier around ground targets, into which enemy bombers would obligingly fly. It was believed a benefit of using the kites would be the ability to deploy them in winds too severe for barrage balloons. The Commanding Officer of the Mullion balloon station was a Mr Long, who had been awarded both the Air Force Medal and the British Empire Medal; in an earlier existence, he had seen service as the first Petty Officer Coxswain on RNAS Mullion's C.9 airship, during the summer of 1916.

2 REMAINS

Today, evidence can still be detected of the former RNAS Mullion. On the eastern side of the site is a windfarm which provides a convenient landmark when making a search. Permission should be sought to visit, as the area is fenced off. The land is still largely scrub though the passing of the years has encouraged the spread of undergrowth. However, both airship shed floors survive, as do signs of some of the roadways, together with a number of the heavy concrete blocks used to help support the windbreaks at the doors of the sheds. Look across the exposed site on a windswept day and

At Crugmeer, buildings survive which were almost certainly constructed as part of the First World War airfield. (Chris Ashworth)

Mullion today. The shed floors are still extant, as are the huge mounting blocks, seen here, used to anchor the windbreak structures. Behind are the wind-farm windmills which act as a marker for the site. In the far distance is the Goonhilly Earth Station. (Author)

imagine the enormous profile of the sheds above the flat landscape, the struggles to control the airships while taking off and landing, the scores of men nursing them in and out of their accommodation, the returned fliers thawing in their wooden huts and above all, the profound remoteness of the base amid the Cornish countryside of eighty years ago.

Evidence of the outstation at Bochym Wood is no longer possible to find. In the Bude area, however, though the outstation has long since gone, two of the large concrete balls formerly used to moor the airships have fortunately been saved, and these are now preserved in private hands. At the RNAS Padstow/Crugmeer site are the remains of several buildings, some almost certainly First World War, others dating from the Second World War when a radio station was built there. On Tresco, concrete foundations can still be detected and the old power house is intact, though the wooden flying-boat slipway has rotted away.

The few remnants of the stations, particularly those still extant at Mullion, are eerie, perhaps because they really do belong to a bygone age. The surviving relics remain as mute tributes to the endeavour of the RNAS men stationed in Cornwall and the Isles of Scilly, who played such a courageous but unsung part in the struggle to keep Britain's sea lanes free of a determined and ruthless enemy.

APPENDIX ONE
RNAS/RAF airfield and airship station command structure in Cornwall
and the Isles of Scilly, to 1919

On 18 December 1916 the Admiralty formed an Anti-Submarine Division, commanded by Rear-Admiral A L Duff, whose responsibilities included the U-boat hunters around the entire British coastline. On 3 April 1917 the resources of the RNAS were reorganised and Mullion became part of the newly-formed RNAS South Western Group, which had its headquarters at Mount Wise, Devonport, and reported to C-in-C HM Ships and Vessels Devonport. The Group was created to control and co-ordinate the activities and resources of the growing RNAS presence in the south-west and south Wales, as those areas assumed an increasingly important role in the anti U-boat campaign.

The officer appointed to command the Group was Wing Commander Eugene L Gerrard. The Newlyn /Land's End, Padstow/Crugmeer and Tresco stations - the latter initially referred to confusingly in RNAS documentation variously as (sic) RNAS Port Melon and RNAS Port Mellon, even following the relocation of the base to its final site - were all placed under the control of the South Western Group. The Group also embraced the aircraft stations at Cattewater (Devon) and Fishguard (Pembroke), together with the airship base at Pembroke, though in November 1917 the two Welsh stations were separated out and formed a new Group under the Senior Naval Officer Milford Haven.

With the formation of the RAF on 1 April 1918, the South Western Group was disbanded and the RAF's No 9 (Operations) Group was formed at Mount Wise, commanding all Cornish airfields (and others). No 71 (Operations) Wing, reporting to No 9 (Operations) Group, was formed at Penzance in August 1918. No 71 (Operations) Wing commanded the stations at Bude, Mullion and its outstations: Newlyn/(Land's End, Padstow/Crugmeer and Tresco, as well as the storage facilities at Tregantle and Withnoe - and also the airfield used by DH.6s at Westward Ho! in Devon. Notwithstanding the transfer of RNAS resources in Cornwall to the RAF, operational activities of these stations there remained in the hands of the Naval authorities situated at Plymouth. Following the Armistice, No 71 (Operations) Wing survived until at least June 1919, but No 9 (Operations) Group disbanded in the summer of that year - probably July.

APPENDIX TWO
Locations of airfields, airship stations and aircraft storage depots in Cornwall and the Isles of Scilly, 1916 - 19

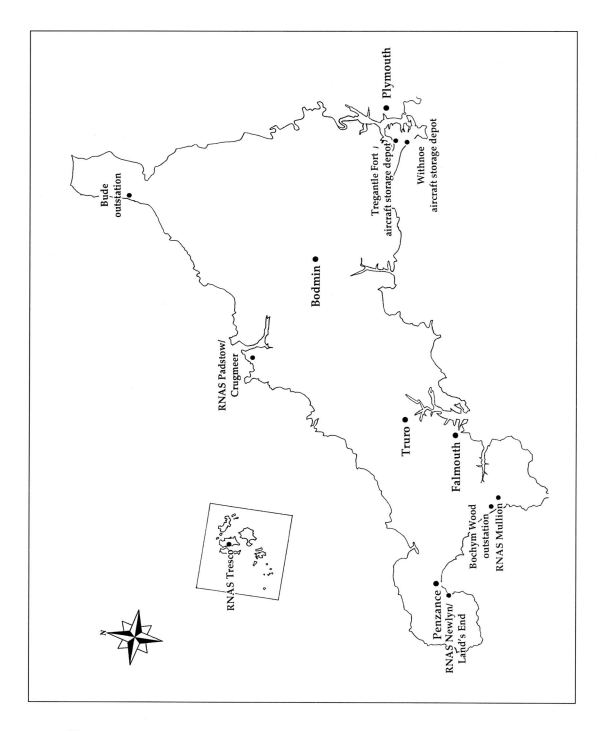

RNAS Mullion 1917

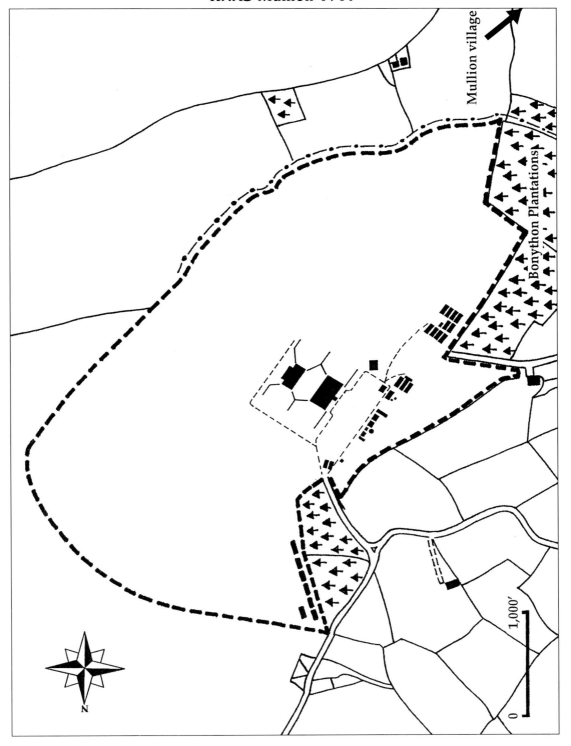

Mullion village

Bonython Plantations

1,000'

0

N

RNAS Newlyn/Land's End 1918

North Pier

South Pier

Newlyn

quarry

1,000'

0

Crugmeer

1,000'

0

RNAS Tresco 1918

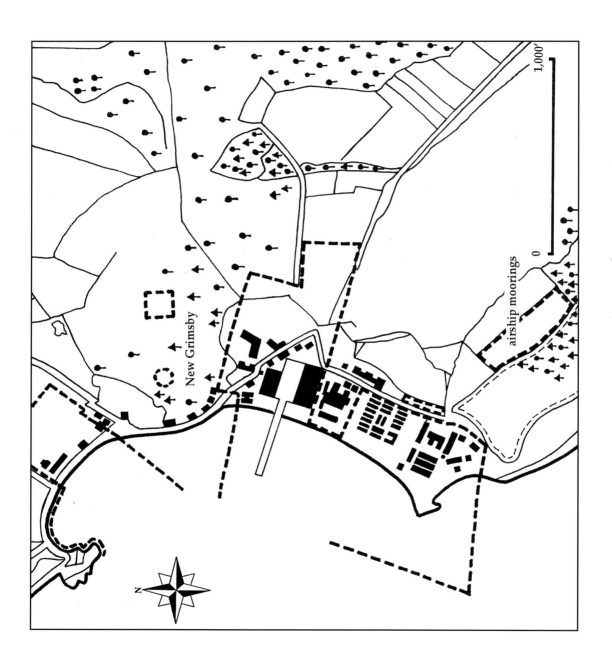

New Grimsby

airship moorings

1,000'

0

APPENDIX THREE
Summary of aircraft Flights and Squadrons
operating from Cornwall and the Isles of Scilly, 1917 - 19,

RNAS Mullion

No 515 (Special Duty - DH.6), No 493 (Light Bomber -DH.9) and No 516 (Special Duty - DH.6) Flights, formed 16 May 1918, 30 May 1918 and 6 June 1918 respectively, within No 254 Squadron, but to No 236 Squadron 20 August 1918, when Squadron formed. Squadron disbanded 15 May 1919.

RNAS Newlyn/Land's End

No 424 and No 425 (Seaplane) Flights (both Short 184) formed 30 May 1918, in No 235 Squadron from 20 August 1918, when Squadron formed. Squadron disbanded 22 February 1919.

RNAS Padstow/Crugmeer

DH.9 Flight formed 2 May 1918, became No 494 (Light Bomber) Flight in No 250 Squadron from 30 May 1918. No 500 and No 501 (Special Duty) Flights (both DH.6) formed 30 May 1918, in No 250 Squadron. Squadron disbanded 15 May 1919.

RNAS Tresco

Nos 350 - 353 Flights (intermingled H12, H.12B, F.3 and Short 184 - also possibly a very small number of FBA training flying-boats) formed on 31 May, 30 June, 15 September and 30 September respectively. In No 234 Squadron from 20 August 1918, when Squadron formed. Squadron disbanded 15 May 1919.

APPENDIX FOUR
Individual aircraft known to have operated from Cornwall
and the Isles of Scilly, 1917 - 19

Sopwith 1½ Strutter
Serial numbers:
N5601, N5602, N5603, N5604 (single-seat bomber variant)
N5607, N5608, N5619, N5623, N5624 (two-seat fighter variant)
Total: 9

de Havilland DH.6
Serial numbers:
B2818, B2847, B2848, B2851, B2852, B2857, B2889, B2896, B2897, B2964, B2965, B2966, C2114, C5166, C5190, C5191, C5192, C5193, C5194, C5205, C5206, C5207, C5706, C6516, C6519, C6561, C6563, C6588, C6661, C6664, C6666, C6667, C6678, C6679, C6680, C6681, C6682, C6683, C7413, C7613, C7645, C7647, C7649, C7663, C7666, C7681, C7799, C7832, C7834, C7836, C7838, C7840, C7842, C7843, C7844, C7846, C7847, C7848, C7849, C7850, C7851, C7852, C7853, C7854, C7855, C7856, C7857, C7858, C7859
Total: 69
Also, the following examples stored at Tregantle (ex-Royal Flying Corps): B2944, B2945, B2946, B2947, B2948, B2949
Total: 6

de Havilland DH.9
Serial numbers:
B7611, B7612, B7613, B7639, B7640, B7662, B7663, B7665, B7666, C1300, C1301, C1302, C1303, C1304, C1305, C1306, C1387, D1711, D1712, D1713, D1714, D2963, D2964, D2965, D2966, D2968, D2969, D5754, H4284, H4287
Total: 30

Short 184
Serial numbers:
8025, 8042, 8049, 8350, 8355, 9059, 9092, N1086, N1143*, N1146, N1149, N1240, N1242, N1254, N1255, N1601, N1604, N1605, N1606, N1607, N1609, N1612, N1614, N1616, N1618, N1620, N1622, N1624, N1635, N1636, N1743, N1767, N1770, N1785, N1824, N2631, N2797, N2798, N2799, N2828, N2919, N2924, N2926, N2954, N2955, N2958, N2959, N2960, N2961, N2962, N2963, N2979, N2988, N2989
Total: 50
* Ground instructional use only, Tresco, arrived March 1918

Parnall-built Fairey Hamble Baby
Serial numbers:
N1191, N1205
Total: 2

Curtiss H.12
Serial numbers:
8652, 8653, 8654, 8656, 8664, 8665, 8674, 8675, 8678, 8680, 8686, N4341
Total: 12

Felixstowe F.3
Serial numbers:
N4000, N4001, N4002, N4234, N4238, N4240, N4241, N4243, N4413, N4415
Total: 10

For study of the service histories of the above aircraft, the reader is commended to the book *Royal Navy Aircraft Serials and Units* 1911 - 1919 by Ray Sturtivant and Gordon Page, published by Air-Britain, 1992.

APPENDIX FIVE
Individual airships operating from RNAS Mullion, 1916 - 1919

Type	Period of service
C Class:	
C.2	April 1917 - December 1918
C.9	June 1916 - October 1918
C.10	June 1916 - October 1916 (first flight Mullion, August 1916)
C.22	October 1916 - March 1917
C.23a	September 1917 - May 1918
SSZ Class:	
SSZ.14	July 1917 - October 1918 (struck off Mullion October 1919)
SSZ.15	August 1917 - April 1918
SSZ.25	December 1917 - January 1918
SSZ.27	March 1918 - December 1918
SSZ.40	April 1918 - January 1919
SSZ.42	May 1918 - November 1918
SSZ.45	May 1918 - November 1918
SSZ.47	May 1918 - November 1918
SSZ.49	June 1918 - September 1918
SSZ.75	November 1918 - December 1918
C* Class:	
C*6	May 1918 - November 1918
C*10	July 1918 - November 1918
Other types:	
SSE.2 *Mullion Twin*	March 1918 - January 1919

Other movements:
C.6 crash-landed near Mullion on 2 December 1916 while based at RNAS Pembroke.
SST.2 is known to have visited Bochym Wood out-station from its usual post at Toller.

RNAS Tresco – sorties by individual aircraft

Aircraft Type	Serial Number	Date of First Patrol	4.17	5.17	6.17	7.17	8.17	9.17	10.17	11.17	12.17	1.18	2.18	3.18	4.18	5.18	6.18	7.18	8.18	9.18	10.18	Total Sorties (Scillies)	Total Flying Hours (Scillies)	Remarks
H.12	8654	13.04.17	6	12	2		2	1														23	63.57	20.05.18 worn out
H.12	8656	13.04.17	8	11	2			18	1	2												42	77.12	In commission. Vee hull fitted after 101hrs
H.12	8665	20.04.17	8	1	5	2																16	46.24	16.12.17 lost from moorings in gale
H.12	8664	21.04.17	7	3																		10	27.49	09.05.17 wrecked in gale. Three crew killed
H.12	8674	04.06.17			10	13				1												24	56.22	28.02.18 broke adrift from mooring in gale, wrecked on rocks
H.12	8680	12.06.17				8	8		10	5	4											35	29.49	16.12.17 lost from moorings in gale
H.12	8686	14.06.17				1	7		4		1											13	29.49	16.12.17 lost from moorings in gale
H.12	N4341	23.03.18												8	14	15	11	9	23	3	2	85	239.22	In commission
H.12	8675	17.05.18														14	11					25	57.4	15.06.18 lost at sea, presumed crankshaft failure. W/T lost
F.3	N4243	04.06.18															17	12	12	1	1	43	123.25	In commission
F.3	N4238	06.06.18															3	8	5	3		19	43.57	In commission - soggy
F.3	N4234	05.07.18																6				6	17.28	08.07.18 lost in tow, crew safe
F.3	N4000	20.07.18																1				1	13	Hull wrecked prior to first flight, struck rocks getting off, awaiting repair
F.3	N4001	13.08.18																	3			3	5.2	22.08.18 lost at sea, starboard engine failure, crew saved
F.3	N4241	08.08.18																	3			3	52.21	In commission - soggy
F.3	N4240	07.09.18																	13		3	16	12.25	In commission - weak type hull
F.3	N4002	25.09.18																		4		4	15.5	In commission
F.3	N4412	25.09.18																		3	3	6	2	In commission
F.3	N4415	11.10.18																			1	1	1.45	In commission
																					373	**931.99**	

	4.17	5.17	6.17	7.17	8.17	9.17	10.17	11.17	12.17	1.18	2.18	3.18	4.18	5.18	6.18	7.18	8.18	9.18	10.18
Sorties per Month	29	17	19	24	17	15	15	7	5	1	0	8	14	29	42	56	15	10	5
Aircraft in use per Month	4	4	4	4	3	2	3	2	2	1	0	1	1	2	4	5	6	5	

Tresco-based H.12s 8652, 8653 and 8678: no mention

Source: PRO AIR1/6A?/24/29 - contemporary RNAS record for period 13.04.17 - 12.10.18

APPENDIX SEVEN
Areas patrolled by RNAS aircraft and airships operating from
Cornwall and the Isles of Scilly

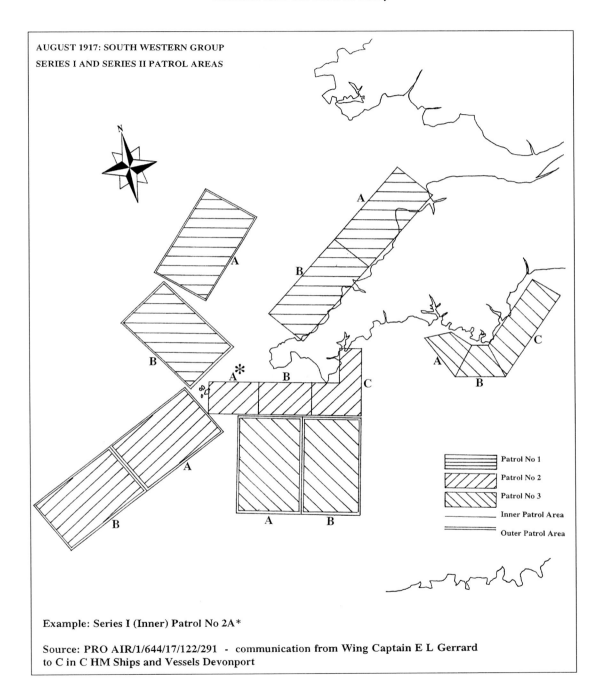

AUGUST 1917: SOUTH WESTERN GROUP
SERIES I AND SERIES II PATROL AREAS

Patrol No 1
Patrol No 2
Patrol No 3
Inner Patrol Area
Outer Patrol Area

Example: Series I (Inner) Patrol No 2A*

Source: PRO AIR/1/644/17/122/291 - communication from Wing Captain E L Gerrard
to C in C HM Ships and Vessels Devonport

RNAS rank structure, and Royal Flying Corps equivalents

RNAS 1912 - 18

RFC 1912 - 1918 (and RAF 1918 - 19)

Commissioned Officers:

	General
	Lieutenant General
	Major General
	Brigadier
Wing Captain	Colonel
Wing Commander	Lieutenant Colonel
Squadron Commander	Major
Flight Lieutenant	Captain
Flight Sub-Lieutenant	Lieutenant
	Second Lieutenant

Non-Commissioned Officers and other Ranks:

Chief Petty Officer I	Warrant Officer
Chief Petty Officer II	Quartermaster-Sergeant
Chief Petty Officer III	Flight Sergeant
Petty Officer	Sergeant
Leading Mechanic	Corporal
Air Mechanic I	Air Mechanic I
Acting Air Mechanic I	Air Mechanic II
Air Mechanic II	Air Mechanic III

APPENDIX NINE
Specifications of airship types operating from Cornwall, 1916 - 19

Coastal Class Airship

Powerplant:	One 150 hp Sunbeam (tractor), plus one 220 hp Renault (pusher)		
Overall length:	196 ft	**Overall height:**	52 ft 1 in
Overall width:	9 ft 6 in	**Envelope capacity:**	170,000 cu ft
Ballonet capacity:	51,000 cu ft		
Maximum speed:	47 mph	**Maximum endurance:**	up to 21 hours
Armament:	Up to four .303 in Lewis machine-guns		
	Four 112 lb, or two 230 lb bombs, or depth charges		

Coastal Star Class Airship

Powerplant:	One 110 hp Beliet (tractor), plus one 220 Renault or one 240hp Fiat (pusher)		
Overall length:	217 ft	**Overall height:**	55 ft 9 in
Overall width:	50 ft	**Envelope capacity:**	210,000 cu ft
Ballonet capacity:	68,860 cu ft		
Maximum speed:	56 mph		
Armament:	Up to four .303 in Lewis machine-guns mounted on car		
	Two 100 lb bombs plus two 230 lb bombs		

SSZ Class Airship

Powerplant:	One 75 hp Rolls-Royce Hawk		
Overall length:	143 ft	**Overall height:**	47 ft
Overall width:	39 ft 6 in	**Envelope capacity:**	70,000 cu ft
Ballonet capacity:	19,600 cu ft	**Maximum speed:**	53 mph
Maximum rate of climb: 1,200 ft/min			
Armament:	One .303 in Lewis machine-gun		
	Four 110 lb, or two 230 lb bombs		

SSE.2 *Mullion Twin* Airship

Powerplant:	Two 75 hp Rolls Royce Hawk		
Envelope capacity:			
(original)	85,000 cu ft		
(eventual)	100,000 cu ft		
Maximum speed:	55 mph	**Endurance:**	30 hours at 42 mph

Specifications of aircraft types operating from Cornwall
and the Isles of Scilly, 1916 - 19

Sopwith 1½ Strutter
Powerplant: One 110 hp Clerget 9Z, or 130 hp Clerget 9B
Dimensions: Span 33 ft 6 in   Length 25 ft 3 in
             Height 10 ft 3 in   Wing area 346 sq ft
Weights (110 hp Clerget):   Tare 1,259 lb   All-up 2,149 lb
Performance (110 hp Clerget): Maximum speed 106 mph at sea level
             Climb, 10 min 50 sec to 6,500 ft
             Endurance 4½ hours
Armament: One .303 in Vickers machine-gun, two 65 lb bombs

de Havilland DH.6
Powerplant: One 90 hp RAF.1a, or 90 hp Curtiss OX-2 or OX-5, or 80 hp Renault
Dimensions: Span 35 ft 11¼in   Length 27 ft 3½ in
             Height 10 ft 9½ in   Wing area 436.3 sq ft
Weights: Tare 1,460 lb   All-up 2,027 lb
Performance: Maximum speed 75 mph at 2,000 ft, 66 mph at 6,500 ft
             Climb, 35 min to 6,500 ft
             Service ceiling 6,500 ft
             Endurance 2½ hours
Armament: Maximum bombload 100 lb

de Havilland DH.9
Powerplant: One 230 hp BHP or Siddeley Puma, or 230 hp Galloway Adriatic, or 260 hp Fiat A.12
Dimensions: Span 42 ft 4½ in   Length 30 ft 6 in
             Height 11 ft 2 in   Wing area 434 sq ft
Weights (Puma): Tare 2,203 lb   All-up 3,669 lb
Performance (Puma): Maximum speed 111.5 mph at 10,000 ft
             Climb, 1 min 25 sec to 1,000 ft
             Service ceiling 15,500 ft
             Endurance 4½ hours
Armament: One .303 in Vickers forward-firing Vickers machine gun
             One or two .303 in Lewis machine-gun firing aft
             Two 230 lb or four 112 b bombs

Short 184
Powerplant: One 225 hp, or 240 hp, or 260 hp, or 275 hp Sunbeam, or 240 hp Renault, or 250 hp
             Rolls-Royce Eagle
Dimensions: Span 63 ft 6¼ in   Length 40 ft 7½ in
             Height 13 ft 6 in   Wing area 688 sq ft
Weights (260 hp Sunbeam):   Tare 3,703 lb   All-up 5,363 lb
Performance(260 hp Sunbeam): Maximum speed 88.5 mph at 2,000 ft
             Climb, 8 min 32 sec to 2,000 ft
             Service ceiling 9,000 ft
             Endurance 2½ hours
Armament: One .303 in Lewis machine-gun firing aft
             Maximum bombload of 585 lb, or one 14-in torpedo

Parnall-built Fairey Hamble Baby
Powerplant: One 110 hp Clerget, or 130 hp Clerget
Dimensions: Span 27 ft 9¼   Length 23 ft 4 in
                           Height 9 ft 6 in   Wing area 246 sq ft
Weights (110 hp Clerget):   Tare 1,386 lb   All-up 1,946 lb
Performance: Maximum speed 90 mph at 2,000 ft
                           Climb, 5 min 30 sec to 2,000 ft
                           Service ceiling 7,600 ft
                           Endurance 2 hours
Armament: One .303 in Lewis machine-gun, two 65 lb bombs

Curtiss H.12
Powerplant: Two 275 hp Rolls-Royce Eagle I. Later, two 345 hp Eagle VII or 375 hp Eagle VIII
Dimensions: Span 92 ft 8½ in   Length 46 ft 6 in
                           Height 16 ft 6 in   Wing area 1,216 sq ft
Weights: Tare 7,293 lb   All-up 10,650 lb
Performance: Maximum speed 85 mph at 2,000 ft
                           Climb, 3 min 20 sec to 2,000 ft
                           Service ceiling 10,800 ft
                           Endurance 6 hours
Armament: Up to four .303 in Lewis machine-guns on flexible mountings
                           Four 100 lb or two 230 lb bombs

Felixstowe F.3
Powerplant: Two 345 hp Rolls-Royce Eagle VIII
Dimensions: Span 102 ft   Length 49 ft 2 in
                           Height 18 ft 8 in   Wing area 1,432 sq ft
Weights: Tare 7,958 lb   All-up (normal) 12,235 lb
                           All-up (max) 13,281 lb
Performance: Maximum speed 93 mph at 2,000 ft
                           Climb, 5 min 15 sec to 2,000 ft
                           Service ceiling 12,500 ft (light load)
                           Endurance (maximum) 9½ hours
Armament: Four .303 in Lewis machine-guns in nose, upper rear
                           cockpit and two waist positions
                           Two 230 lb bombs